Beyond the Chocolate Window

Daily readings and meditations for Advent and Christmas

Becky Lovatt

Onwards and Upwards Publishers

3 Radfords Turf, Cranbrook, Exeter,
EX5 7DX, United Kingdom.

www.onwardsandupwards.org

This first edition published in the United Kingdom by Onwards and Upwards Publishers (2018).

ISBN:	978-1-78815-633-2
Illustrations / cover:	Sara Holden
Graphic design:	LM Graphic Design
Typeface:	Sabon LT

Printed in the United Kingdom.

About the Author

Becky Lovatt is a Methodist deacon living and working in East Devon. She holds a master's degree in Theology and Ministry and is passionate about reaching out to those on the margins of traditional church.

Becky is very proud of her Cornish roots and enjoys returning home when she can, to take in the beauty of the coastline. Having been brought up in a Christian family, her faith took on new meaning in 1994 when she began to work at Camp Stapleton, a camp for underprivileged girls in Detroit, USA. Here Becky met with God and received a call into full-time ordained ministry.

Becky is married to Tim, and they have a son, Theo, who is their pride and joy. In 2013 Becky published her first book of meditations for Lent and Holy Week entitled *In the Shadows of Victory: Ride the Rollercoaster of Holy Week*. Through the sales of this book, she was able to raise money for the Baby Special Care Unit at the Royal Berkshire Hospital, in Reading, in memory of their stillborn baby girl, Emerald.

Acknowledgements

My grateful thanks go to:

Sara Holden,
who illustrated this book;

Reg Ammon, and Gordon and Sharon Howe,
who painstakingly proof-read all I wrote;

the Methodist Church,
for giving me a sabbatical to complete this work;

and to the many people who have helped and encouraged me
in thought, word and prayer throughout the whole venture.

Dedicated to Tim and Theo,
without whose love and support
this book would never have been written.

My thanks also go to all those that have
encouraged me along the way,
both mentally and spiritually.

Contents

Preface

I want to invite you to join me on a journey – a journey through the Bible, from beginning to end. I want to explore the thoughts and feelings of some of the people touched by God, so that you might experience the same.

In our house Advent is a time when the excitement of Christmas begins to build. The shops are stocked, the TV advertisements are in overdrive and the windows of the Advent calendar reveal each day another chocolate delight.

I want to look beyond the windows of a chocolate Advent calendar; to stand in the shoes of the characters who influenced, experienced and benefited from the very first Advent, Christmas and beyond; to stand with those whose lives were changed in and through the person of Jesus Christ, so that our lives might also be changed.

This book presents daily meditations, offering new insights into well-known stories. Unlike many Advent meditations, it does not end abruptly on Christmas Day but continues through the twelve days of Christmas to put the Advent hope into its proper context.

Each meditation is accompanied by a relevant extract from scripture which, for the sake of consistency, have all been taken from the New Revised Standard Version of the Bible. With each meditation, there are three questions offered for reflection, an action which may be undertaken to aid contemplation, and a closing prayer.

The book is divided into three sections:

- *The Hope Foretold.*
  During the first two weeks of Advent, we will look at how the Old Testament prepares for the coming of Jesus.
- *The Hope Realised.*
  During the second two weeks of Advent, we will view the Christmas story through the eyes of characters who would have experienced the events first-hand.
- *The Hope to Come.*
  During the twelve days of Christmas, we will see what impact Jesus' life had on the world.

Although the meditations in this book are all based on biblical events, I have added names and details not necessarily offered to us from the scriptures alone. The stories told in this book include a certain degree of personal interpretation.

My prayer is that this book might enable you to get to grips with the 'waiting' and the 'preparation' aspects of Advent; that you might be able to look beyond the Advent calendar windows, and beyond the chocolate, and explore a deeper, more intimate relationship with God through his son, Jesus Christ.

Foreword by Rev. Dr Jonathan H. Pye

In the busyness of contemporary life, few people today find the time to pause and to use the periods of preparation and reflection that the cycle and rhythm of the Christian year offers in order to prepare properly for the great festivals of the Christian calendar, and so all too often they arrive at Christmas or Easter rushed and unprepared. As a consequence, they find that their appreciation of the 'high moments' of the Christian year to which such seasons point is diminished. Like so much in life, our willingness to prepare properly determines the quality of the final outcome.

Our preparedness to walk with our Lord rather than running ahead, to sweep the corners of our lives rather than neglecting the details, and to make ready our hearts in Advent or Lent respectively rather than being caught up in the pervasive consumerism that marks our modern age, will have a profound effect on our ability to experience, and understand, those points to which these journeys of faith and devotion lead us.

At a time when so much of life is fragmented and fragmentary, a consequence of the post-modern mindset, rediscovering the threads that connect is a vital way of rebalancing life and of discovering that the arrival and the journey are both intimately and inextricably linked.

This is a book that is refreshingly contemporary in its style, yet it also draws from the deep wells of the great historic traditions of Christian spirituality – the engagement with scripture of the Benedictines, the exercises of the Ignation Tradition, the focused aphorisms of the Desert Fathers and Mothers, the groundedness of the Celtic saints. It is thus, in equal measure, a book that is deep but accessible, both theological and practical, prayerful yet including helpful activities, born out of a life of Christian practice as it is lived in daily experience and as it is reflected upon.

Whether it is used by an individual or as a resource for use with others, in this profound little book Becky Lovatt helps us to navigate Advent with its twin themes of Hope and Judgement in ways that are designed to help even the most busy among us to pause, to ponder and to share the journey, so that our arrival might be the moment of wonder by which we are astonished but one for which we are nonetheless prepared and so can recognise it for what it is.

Rev. Dr Jonathan H. Pye
Chair, Bristol District of the Methodist Church

Opening Prayer

The following prayer could be said before each day's meditation. This will add a sense of continuity as you journey through Advent, once again preparing to meet the coming of the king in and through the birth of Jesus Christ, and through his life, death and resurrection.

Adoration

Eternal God,
You are the source of all life,
You are fountain of all wisdom
And you are the safe harbour of all grace.
Your days are endless
And your mercies never cease.

I depend on you, as all the world belongs to you.
I trust you, and once again offer my life to you,
as Jesus laid down his life for us.

Lord, open my eyes that I might see Jesus.
Open my ears that I might hear his voice.
Open my heart that I might know the heart of Christ.
To the glory of his name now and forever.
Amen.

Confession

Lord, forgive me…
for the times I have fallen short of your glory;
for the times I have failed to put you first;
for the times when my own pride has got in the way;
for the times I have spoken when I should have remained silent;
for the times I have neglected to stand up for justice
and speak out against oppression.

Lord, forgive me.
You, O God, are a God of mercy and grace,
    and if I come to you and humbly confess my sins,
    I believe that I will be forgiven.
    Therefore, I hear your words of grace:
    "Your sins are forgiven."

Thank you, God.
Amen.

Prayers for Others

Take some time to prayer for the needs of others:

- *for the world;*
- *for your country;*
- *for your local community;*
- *for the church both nationally and locally;*
- *for your family;*
- *for yourself.*

After each prayer, you may wish to say:

Lord, in your mercy, hear my prayer.

At the end, you could also say the Lord's Prayer, if you wish:

Our Father,
Who art in heaven,
Hallowed be thy name.
Thy kingdom come.
Thy will be done,
On earth, as it is in heaven.
Give us this day our daily bread.
And forgive us our trespasses,
As we forgive those that trespass against us.
And lead us not into temptation,
But deliver us from evil.
For thine is the kingdom,
The power, and the glory,
For ever and ever. Amen.

The Hope Foretold

A Way to Prepare

Pull up the weeds.
Grab them by the roots,
Wiggle them a bit,
And pull them up.
Clear the group
    for the lawnmower.
Make it ready.
Feel the rain,
Not just light spots but torrents.
Hear the thunder,
Not just distant rumbles
But a storm overhead.
A reflection on life.
Prepare the way,
Make it straight,
Make it ready –
But it isn't always easy.

Sometimes
We get rained on,
Ignored,
Left out in the cold,
Tired and wet,
Frustrated and angry.
Yet, it is then that
    we must stop and consider:
Who am I?
What have I been asked to do?
So laugh,
Smile,
Get warm;
Reflect on God and start again,
For there is a way to prepare
And a path to make ready –
    for Christ.

1st Sunday of Advent

Light in the Darkness

Bible Reading

Again Jesus spoke to them, saying, "I am the light of the world. Whoever follows me will never walk in darkness but will have the light of life." Then the Pharisees said to him, "You are testifying on your own behalf; your testimony is not valid." Jesus answered, "Even if I testify on my own behalf, my testimony is valid because I know where I have come from and where I am going, but you do not know where I come from or where I am going. You judge by human standards; I judge no one. Yet even if I do judge, my judgment is valid; for it is not I alone who judge, but I and the Father who sent me. In your law it is written that the testimony of two witnesses is valid. I testify on my own behalf, and the Father who sent me testifies on my behalf."

John 8:12-18

The Voice of Hope

Jesus says:

"Do not be afraid. I am the light in the darkness; the voice of hope, in the midst of despair.

"At the beginning of time, as one – Father, Son, and Spirit – we spoke creation into being. God uttered. The Son become the Word that was spoken. And the Spirit of wisdom hovered over the waters.

"In the beginning, there was nothing; chaos ruled, and darkness covered the whole earth. Yet, item by item, day by day, millennium by millennium, life came into existence – breath from breath, bone from bone, being from being. Hope was alive.

"I am the gate to the good pastures; and I am the shepherd who will gather the scattered flock. I am the bread to feed the hungry and the living water of new life. Follow me and be guided by my voice: the voice of hope that will rally the remnants of God's people and build a new nation. It will be a nation not built on location or with bricks, but a movement built on love, where justice and peace are the driving force. I am the hope for the hopeless, the candle in the darkened room. I offer an open invitation into a personal relationship with the Almighty.

"Still, after all these years, after everything – after God became human and lived among his people; after God was hailed as king, then betrayed, rejected, denied and crucified; after he was raised to life, to sit on his rightful throne in glory – even now, the darkness lingers on. The bombs still fall. Brother still raises arms against brother and the blackness of hate still penetrates the light.

"Yet, it does not have to. Shine, light, shine! Do not let the darkness claim the victory. Do not allow the hope to be squeezed out. For I am the light – claim it for yourself and banish the darkness once and for all.

"Come with me on a journey – a journey of hope and acceptance, where you will be valued and claimed as children of God. Come and enter into my new kingdom – a kingdom where I am the king, and where all people are judged as equal, where God is friend and loving father.

"Come and let me light a candle for you. I will be your light, your peace and your hope."

Pause for Thought

- Jesus offers 'light' and 'hope'. What do you think that means, and how could you respond to that today?
- How do you feel about approaching the creator of the universe?
- We are all on the journey with God. Where do you see yourself on that journey at the moment?

Action

If you have a candle at home, light it and ponder Jesus' claim that he was (and is) the light of the world, who came to offer hope and light.

Prayer

Light of the world,
shine your light wherever there is darkness in my life;
bring hope to the hopeless and joy to all hearts.
Help me to be salt and light to those around me
and walk in support of all people in their journey with God.
Amen.

WEEK 1, MONDAY

We Ate the Apple

Bible Reading

So God created humankind in his image, in the image of God he created them; male and female he created them.

Genesis 1:27

And the rib that the Lord God had taken from the man he made into a woman and brought her to the man. Then the man said, "This at last is bone of my bones and flesh of my flesh; this one shall be called Woman, for out of Man this one was taken."

Genesis 2:22-25

If you have time, read the whole passage in Genesis 3:1-24.

The Voice of Eve

I guess you could say that humanity's downfall began with us – Adam and me, and that wretched snake. If it hadn't been for the snake, everything would have been fine. Well... that's what I like to tell myself, anyway.

God created heaven and earth, and sea and sky. Then God made Adam, and from Adam he fashioned me. He set us both over and above all the other animals and plants he had formed.

"Roam in my garden," he told us. "Make it your own; name the beasts and flowers for me. Just don't eat from the tree in the middle."

We had so much to choose from – the whole garden was ours – and yet I was drawn to the one tree we were told to keep clear of. I was attracted, it's true. Somehow, it seemed to draw me to itself, almost as if it was silently calling my name. However, I am sure I could have stayed strong – *if only it hadn't been for that snake.*

The creature goaded me, tempting me. It told me all kinds of untruths about how God wouldn't know – or wouldn't mind. I fell for it, hook, line and sinker.

It would not have been so bad if I had left it there, but I didn't. I got Adam involved as well. I became the tempter – the 'devil on his shoulder', the barbed wire pricking at his skin.

Before long we had both eaten from the tree whose fruit had been forbidden. Suddenly, our eyes were opened; we recognised our naked bodies. We had become like God, with the knowledge of good and evil.

We heard our creator coming, walking in the cool of the evening. We hid, but God called to us. "Come close, my children, and walk with me," he said.

When we finally appeared, our father knew that we had betrayed him. He knew instantly that we had eaten from the tree. We had to come clean and confess to what we had done.

Adam blamed me. I blamed the snake. Yet each of us had to endure the punishment. The snake and all his kind were sentenced to crawl on their bellies and eat dust for the rest of their existence. I, and all of womankind, would experience pain in childbirth. Adam, and all mankind, would have to work hard their whole lives in order to eat, and would ultimately die.

We were banished from the garden – left to go our own way and fend for ourselves. We had become separated from God – a wedge driven between us; a wound that could only be healed though another's life laid down and a sacrifice made. The tempter had gained the upper hand; God, it seemed, had been defeated.

However, we were cradled in love. Even though we had been so easily lured, God did not *abandon* us. We had children of our own. They grew into a strong and powerful race that populated the earth. We had eaten from the tree of knowledge and opened a crack that would become a chasm, a void between God's people and their creator. Even then, there was a plan in place – a plan for repentance, for healing and for grace.

Pause for Thought

- Can you remember an occasion when you felt strongly tempted to do something you knew you shouldn't?
- Have you ever, like Adam and Eve, let people (or God) down, yet tried to blame others?
- Do you believe that Jesus and his life and death were part of the plan from the very beginning? Why?

Action

The next time you eat a piece of fruit, imagine what it might have been like for Eve to be tempted by the snake into eating the fruit of the forbidden tree.

Then think about what temptation looks like in today's world – do you find people (or advertising, media etc.) tempting you to do things you know you shouldn't?

Prayer

Creator God,
help me not to succumb to the temptations I face on earth
and to keep my eyes fixed on the goals of heaven.
When I *am* tempted, keep me strong;
and if I fail, remind me that I am still loved
and cared for by you.
Amen.

Week 1, Tuesday

A Life of Waiting

Bible Reading

Now the Lord said to Abram, "Go from your country and your kindred and your father's house to the land that I will show you. I will make of you a great nation, and I will bless you, and make your name great, so that you will be a blessing. I will bless those who bless you, and the one who curses you I will curse; and in you all the families of the earth shall be blessed." So Abram went, as the Lord had told him; and Lot went with him. Abram was seventy-five years old when he departed from Haran.

Genesis 12:1-4

If you have time, you could also read Genesis 17:5 and 18:10-12.

The Voice of Abraham

What a life I have led! A life of waiting – waiting on God, the author and protector of my life and of my faith. I am old, and I have waited all my days. I am still waiting.

I remember the beginning as if it were yesterday. I wasn't young then. Some might even say I was 'over the hill' to start with. However, God plucked me out of my security and set me on a journey of discovery and hope.

I was spoken to by the God of my youth. "Leave everything," he said, "your country, your extended family and your father's home. Leave everything! I will show you a new land. I will make you into a great nation, and I will bless you and all those you know. Leave everything!"

So, I left. Well, that's not *exactly* true. I mumbled and I grumbled, and I tried to do everything in my power to walk away. However, God did not stop. He kept on calling, and I kept on waiting for it all to pass – but it didn't.

We argued – God and I – but he is God, and there was only ever going to be one winner. So, eventually I left, leaving everything behind me as I had been instructed to do.

Sarah, my wife, came with me, and my nephew, Lot. We travelled together, waiting every moment on God's provision. Lot and I began to argue. He wanted one thing and I wanted what God wanted. More waiting… for Lot to leave and for my next instruction.

It came in the form of a promise. God told me not to be afraid; that he would be my shield and my great reward. I was terrified, and every day of waiting played tricks on my mind. He promised I would be the father of a great nation and that my descendants would populate the earth. Yet, how could this be? Sarah couldn't have children, and with every day that passed, I was getting older.

Years later, some visitors arrived. I welcomed them. Sarah cooked up a storm – and then they broke their news.

"You're going to have a child," they said.

You could have knocked me down with a feather – and Sarah, well, she could not contain her laughter.

After more waiting, we did have a son, just as God had said. We named him Isaac, and he grew big and strong. God wanted to test my faithfulness and asked me to sacrifice him – but that's not my story to tell.

More years of waiting, then I lost Sarah. She was my rock and my confidence. She was called home to be with God, and I was left to wait alone.

Now I wait for death. My sons have grown and have sons of their own. Thus, the nation that God has promised will come into being – a nation from which will rise up a great king, equal to God himself, who will rule the kingdom of God as God intended.

Pause for Thought

- Abraham spent his whole life waiting. Advent is about waiting too. How will you prepare to wait for the coming king this year?

- God was faithful to his promises to Abraham. How have you experienced God's faithfulness in your own life? Thank him for that today.
- Abraham was asked to leave everything. Is there something God might be calling you to do? How can you respond?

Action

The next time you make yourself a hot drink, think about the steps you take – getting cups out, putting teabags in the teapot, checking there is enough sugar in the bowl, etc.

Preparation is important, and it is the same with Advent. We wait and prepare for the birth of Jesus.

While you enjoy your hot drink, maybe you could spend a moment to think again about how you will prepare to welcome King Jesus.

Prayer

God of Abraham,
    thank you that you are close to me
    as I wait for you to 'break through' in my life.
Help me to wait on you with faith and confidence,
    and to put my trust in your unfailing love.
Stand with me even as I wait on you.
In the name of Jesus, I ask.
Amen.

WEEK 1, WEDNESDAY

How Dare You!

Bible Reading

After these things God tested Abraham. He said to him, "Abraham!" And he said, "Here I am." He said, "Take your son, your only son Isaac, whom you love, and go to the land of Moriah, and offer him there as a burnt offering on one of the mountains that I shall show you. ... When they came to the place that God had shown him, Abraham built an altar there and laid the wood in order. He bound his son Isaac, and laid him on the altar, on top of the wood. Then Abraham reached out his hand and took the knife to kill his son. But the angel of the Lord called to him from heaven, and said, "Abraham, Abraham!" And he said, "Here I am." He said, "Do not lay your hand on the boy or do anything to him; for now I know that you fear God, since you have not withheld your son, your only son, from me." And Abraham looked up and saw a ram, caught in a thicket by its horns. Abraham went and took the ram and offered it up as a burnt offering instead of his son.

Genesis 22:1-2,9-13

The Voice of Sarah

Waiting?

I'll tell you all about waiting! I waited for years; waited for my husband Abraham to share his life with me; waited for God to fulfil his promise; and now, after all this waiting, *this* happens.

I followed my husband, who followed his God. I left my home, my family and the people I loved. I followed because I believed that I would share in the promise. Eventually, after years of waiting... *it was mine.*

As Abraham's wife, I had been unable to fulfil what it means to be a woman in my culture and time – to bear a child. Yes, I was barren and broken emotionally, physically and spiritually, seemingly abandoned by all I had come to trust in. But then the waiting ended.

God came up trumps. Our son, Isaac, was born and he was... *everything.* He was my whole world. He was the realisation of all that had been, all that was, and all that is still to come. This part of God's promise to my husband had been completed and fulfilled.

So, you can imagine the sheer fear in my heart when I woke one morning to find my bed and Isaac's bed empty. I waited for the two of them to return – the father and the son – to embrace them, to still my racing mind and quell my increasing sense of dread.

Eventually, days later, they did arrive. As Abraham told me his tale, my fear turned to rage. God had been calling again – not to move or change this time, but *to kill;* to kill the promise, to kill the one thing we had waited so long for, *to sacrifice our only son.*

How dare he, this God of grace and mercy who had given us so much? How dare he take it away now? Was this a way to punish me for laughing, for doubting his ability to give us a child in the first place? If it was, then he was a cruel and uncaring God and I wanted to walk away immediately.

Then there was my husband, blindly following the leading of a God he couldn't see. I know he had done it before, but this was different. This was our son. Didn't he think to question? Or at least to discuss it with me? No – God came first, as usual.

My anger was abated as I heard my child's cry. He was still breathing, still needing me. Moreover, his heart was still pumping blood around his body.

God had provided a new sacrifice – not my son, but a ram conveniently caught in a bush, a replacement offering – but what did it all mean?

Pause for Thought

- Have there been times in your life when you have been angry at God?
- What do you think is meant by 'righteous anger'?
- Is there ever a time or place for such anger?

Action

The next time you feel angry with someone or a situation, think about how you might let that anger pass and about offering it to God. Perhaps you could clench your fist to represent the anger, and then gradually unfold your fist as a symbol of releasing it to Jesus.

Prayer

God of all things, of waiting, of promise, of anger and of release,
come close to me now and hold me,
here in the situation of life I find myself.
I pray for all those I know who have lost children:
come alongside them and hold them as they journey on.
I bring before you those I know who feel anger
about what they are experiencing or have experienced;
bring release and hope in their lives.
Amen.

Week 1, Thursday

The Passover Lamb

Bible Reading

For I will pass through the land of Egypt that night, and I will strike down every firstborn in the land of Egypt, both human beings and animals; on all the gods of Egypt I will execute judgments: I am the Lord. The blood shall be a sign for you on the houses where you live: when I see the blood, I will pass over you, and no plague shall destroy you when I strike the land of Egypt. This day shall be a day of remembrance for you. You shall celebrate it as a festival to the Lord; throughout your generations you shall observe it as a perpetual ordinance. Seven days you shall eat unleavened bread; on the first day you shall remove leaven from your houses, for whoever eats leavened bread from the first day until the seventh day shall be cut off from Israel.

Exodus 12:12-15

If you have time, read the whole passage in Exodus 1-12.

The Voice of Moses

As a child I was rescued from death. My mother hid me in a basket, then placed me in the bulrushes growing on the banks of the river.

I was brought up in a royal household, raised as an Egyptian prince, yet Hebrew blood ran through my veins. So, when I saw the way my brothers were being treated, I hit out and committed murder. As a fugitive, I fled the scene – in my mind never to return; but God had other ideas.

I took a job minding the sheep in my father-in-law's field. Then something amazing happened. I saw a bush ablaze with flames – but it was not burning. Then from inside it came a voice. "Take off your shoes,

Moses. You are standing on holy ground. I have heard my people crying in pain, as they struggle under the oppressor's whip. Go to the king and tell him to let my people go."

I wasn't keen; I came up with every excuse I could. But every time I built a wall, God dismantled it, brick by brick.

Before long, I found myself a reluctant messenger of God. My brother Aaron and I were soon in the presence of the king of Egypt. We conveyed God's decree: that slaves would be freed and his people would know deliverance.

Nevertheless, the king's heart was as hard as stone, his mind made up. He was unwavering; he was *not* willing to let God's people go.

God showed his power by sending plagues upon Pharaoh and his people – ten in all, from rivers of blood to frogs and boils. Then came the final one: the deaths of the firstborn sons. Still, he would not yield and would not let God's people go.

God instructed us to get the people ready. He showed them his plan to cut the chains of bondage and set them free. They had to take a male lamb – one without mark or blemish – and sacrifice it at twilight. Next, they were to paint their doorframes with the blood, so that the angel of death that was to come would pass over their homes.

It happened just as God foretold it. The firstborn son of every family in Egypt was slaughtered, including the pharaoh's own son – and then he changed his mind.

"Go," he said, "take the people of your God, and go!"

We led the people and the livestock out of slavery. For years we wandered in the desert – every year retelling the story, as instructed. We ate bitter herbs and bread without yeast, and we sacrificed our Passover ('pass over') lambs. Then eventually we reached the promised land.

Pause for Thought

- What is your reaction to reading the story of the killing of the firstborn sons?
- God heard his people cry out to him in their oppression. How might you, together with God, hear those who are oppressed today?

- God told the people to remember the events of their deliverance every year. For us, Jesus became the ultimate Passover lamb. What does this mean to you?

Action

Try to bake some bread without yeast as God's people did (or buy some matzos from your local supermarket). As you eat it, remember how the angel of death passed over the homes of God's people. Then think about how Jesus became the Passover lamb for us all.

Prayer

God of the Passover,
free me from anything that still binds me,
from anything that still leads me into sin.
Help me recognise that Jesus' death on the cross
paid the price of my sin so that I do not have to.
Help me to bring the message of hope to all those
who have not yet heard it.
Amen.

WEEK 1, FRIDAY

Your God Will Be My God

Bible Reading

But Ruth said, "Do not press me to leave you or to turn back from following you! Where you go, I will go; where you lodge, I will lodge; your people shall be my people, and your God my God. Where you die, I will die – there will I be buried. May the Lord do thus and so to me, and more as well, if even death parts me from you!" When Naomi saw that she was determined to go with her, she said no more to her.

Ruth 1:16-18

You could also read the start of the story in Ruth 1:3-5.

The Voice of Ruth

It began in tragedy, with wailing and the gnashing of teeth, but it did not end there, as God brought forth joy from sorrow, hope from despair. However, the God of Israel blessed me, and a descendent of the child from my womb would fulfil his promise.

My name is Ruth and I greet you from the city of Moab.

I was young when I met my first husband. He was handsome and kind, and it was not long before I fell head over heels in love with him. He had come with his brother and his parents to build a new life in our city. They did this, and we were happy.

It didn't stay that way though. Disease came to our land and gripped it, squeezing the very lifeblood from it, killing many. My husband, his brother and father all died, leaving my mother-in-law Naomi with nothing, barely surviving in a land that wasn't hers.

In desperation she decided to return home, to go back to Bethlehem, and my sister-in-law and I chose to go with her. What would that mean?

The answer was clear; we would have to leave all we had ever known, for the unknown; trading all we had ever believed for a new belief and a new God.

A little way into our journey, Naomi urged us to go back to our families; to start again, to move on, to weigh up what we were really leaving behind.

My sister-in-law turned back, but I could not.

"Let me come with you," I insisted. "Wherever you go, I will go. Wherever you live, I will live. Your people will be my people and your God will be my God."

We travelled back to Judea, but when we arrived we had nothing. People huddled together in groups, pointing at us and making cutting remarks. No one helped. No one offered the hand of friendship. They didn't even give us some food.

Naomi had a distant relative named Boaz though. He was kind and let me gather corn from the sides of his field that the workers had left behind. One day I caught his eye. He smiled at me and we talked. As the days and the weeks wore on, we grew closer. I was encouraged to flirt and... next thing I knew, we were married!

Now I had a new husband, and my new God blessed our union with a son. When he had grown, he become the father of Jesse, who become the father of King David, who founded the family into which the Messiah would be born...

Pause for Thought

- For Ruth, it was out of sorrow that joy came. Have there been times in your life when you have been faced with darkness but found hope?
- Ruth's sister-in-law was not willing to leave her homeland behind. Are there ways in which God might be leading you to leave the comfort of what you know? Are you willing?
- The people of Judea talked in groups about Naomi's return, but no one did anything to help. Are there any people you know who have difficult situations, whom you might be able to help practically in some way?

Action

The next time you are shopping, consider buying an item for a food bank. As you do so, think for a moment about the people who have less than you do – adding something to your basket might really help a family in need. And thank God for all he has provided for you over the years.

Prayer

God of Naomi and Ruth,
    help me to reach out to those around me
    who have found themselves in difficult places.
Help me to walk alongside the lonely, to feed the hungry,
    to shelter the homeless and to love the unloved.
Show me how we might bring hope and love to others
    this Christmas.
Show me how I can forge hope from sorrow in people's lives.
Amen.

Week 1, Saturday

My Soul Cries to the Lord

Bible Reading

The Lord is my shepherd, I shall not want.
He makes me lie down in green pastures;
he leads me beside still waters;
he restores my soul.
He leads me in right paths
for his name's sake.
Even though I walk through the darkest valley,
I fear no evil;
for you are with me;
your rod and your staff –
they comfort me.
You prepare a table before me
in the presence of my enemies;
you anoint my head with oil;
my cup overflows.
Surely goodness and mercy shall follow me
all the days of my life,
and I shall dwell in the house of the Lord
my whole life long.

Psalm 23

If you have time, you could also read a selection from Psalms 7, 19, 25, 59, 95, 121, 122 and 139.

The Voice of David

My walk with God has been varied. I have climbed the highest mountains and I have fallen into the deepest pits of despair. I have ridden on the crest of a wave and I have also crashed and burned. Most of that was of my own doing, of course. Yet through it all, God has been my 'constant' – my comfort, my shelter and my help.

As a boy, I was called and chosen; anointed by a messenger of God and set apart for great things. My brothers (all bigger, stronger and more handsome than me) were passed over and I was chosen. My heart was full of praise for God: how majestic his name is in all the earth; how wonderful it was to be in his service!

I worked in my father's fields as a shepherd boy and I understood the importance of looking after the sheep: caring for their every need; finding them good grass to eat and clean water to drink; keeping them safe and secure. So when God showed me that he would be the shepherd for the nation and we would be his sheep, I understood.

As I grew, he was there, always at my side with a shepherd's rod and staff. He was my comfort, protecting me against my enemies – even the time when I stood before the giant Goliath. When it seemed to me that death was fast approaching, when I found myself in the valley of its shadow, even then I was not alone, for God was watching over me; he was my shield and my hiding place.

I gazed up at the hills, looking for someone to help me, but my help did not come from there. Rather, it came from God. And who better? He made heaven and the whole of the universe!

However, some of the choices I made separated me from his presence, driving a gulf between me and my Lord. I chose death over life again and again. On one occasion I became infatuated with my friend's wife, so much so that I just had to have her for myself. It's so hard to confess this but I actually used my position as king to manipulate the situation in my favour. I sent my friend to war, to fight on the front line, and therefore got him killed. I then justified to myself that as he was now dead, it was acceptable for me to marry his widowed wife. I took her just because I was king and therefore I could. It took a man of God called Nathan to show me the error of my ways. Then, of course, I fell to my knees, recognising that the chasm between me and my God was completely of my own making.

God knows me so well – perfectly, in fact. And he has loved me and sought me out despite my sin. He was the one who originally formed me in my mother's womb, and he knew the choices I would make before I even made them. It's incredible to think about it, but *his design was perfect* – I am wonderfully and awesomely made by him, and I am in precious in his sight.

As long as I live, I want to praise my God with a full and thankful heart. As I often sing, "Let everything that has breath praise the Lord!"

Pause for Thought

- Have you ever found yourself using the power you have to manipulate people or situations around you? If so, do you need to confess that to God now?
- Have you ever been on the receiving end of that, when power has been used against you? How did that make you feel?
- It is so easy to forget to praise God and thank him for all that he has done for us. Is there something you can praise him for today?

Action

During this day, think about things that you are grateful to God for. Then, perhaps at the end of the day, write a list of those items of thanksgiving. Take a moment to praise God for each one.

Prayer

God of all knowledge and grace,
    help me to recognise that you are always with me,
    both in the highs and in the lows of my life.
Help me to use the talents and position you have given me
    for the good of people around me and not for my own benefit.
Help me to walk the days of my life on a path of righteousness
    and to offer your comfort and strength to all those I meet.
Amen.

2ND SUNDAY OF ADVENT

Transformation is Real

Bible Reading

"As the Father has loved me, so I have loved you; abide in my love. If you keep my commandments, you will abide in my love, just as I have kept my Father's commandments and abide in his love. I have said these things to you so that my joy may be in you, and that your joy may be complete. This is my commandment, that you love one another as I have loved you. No one has greater love than this, to lay down one's life for one's friends. You are my friends if you do what I command you. I do not call you servants any longer, because the servant does not know what the master is doing; but I have called you friends, because I have made known to you everything that I have heard from my Father. You did not choose me but I chose you. And I appointed you to go and bear fruit, fruit that will last, so that the Father will give you whatever you ask him in my name. I am giving you these commands so that you may love one another."

John 15:9-17

The Voice of Love

Jesus says:

"I am the voice of love. Therefore, I no longer call you servants. I call you my friends. I want you to see that I am loved by my father in heaven and that he has sent me to love you.

"I came, leaving the love of my father's kingdom, coming to earth to be born as a child. I grew in the love of a human family: a mother who was a handmaiden of her God, and a father who took me as his own, putting his own concerns to one side for the good of others.

"I learnt the scriptures. I understood that they referred directly to me: to the life I would live and death I would die. I knew from the very beginning when the end would come.

"In love I gathered a team around me – a team of twelve, made up of unlikely heroes: the fisherman, the tax collector and the outcast. I drew them to myself as companions on the journey. I tried to mould them, to shape and guide them along the way of love. I wanted to offer new life and total transformation to them, and to all who looked to my father, the Holy Spirit and me for help. I used parables and stories and drew pictures with my words. Still, they did not understand or comprehend my love for them, for all God's people.

"I tried to explain that my death would transform life; that if they lived in me, then I would live in them; that they too would know what it meant to love and be loved. I tried to tell them that I loved them so much that I would lay down my life for them – but they just didn't get it.

"Everything that was foretold came to pass. One of my friends betrayed me, another denied me, and still others ran scared for the hills. I was arrested, tried, beaten and crucified, all in the name of love.

"However, my death was not the end – in fact it was just the beginning, as through it, love grew. From city to city, from nation to nation, the word of love lived on and thrived among the people. I came, I lived, I transformed, I died, I rose again, and now I live on – sharing my love through those who choose to bear my name. As they love – love one another and love God – my life and death will fulfil its purpose."

Pause for Thought

- Why do you think Jesus' disciples didn't understand what he was teaching them?
- In theory, would you be willing to die for your friends? Under what circumstances would you be willing to sacrifice yourself in this way?
- Why do you think Jesus was willing to sacrifice his life for you, even though you were not yet born and he never met you?

Action

Are there some people that you find hard to love? God still loves them. Draw a heart and write their names inside that heart. Then pray that God will help you to see them as he does.

Prayer

God of love,
    I choose today to live in you
    just as you have chosen to live in me.
As I go out today, living in you,
    use me to draw others to you.
Help me to love those around me
    with the unconditional love shown in the person of Christ,
    and help me to listen to your voice of love.
Amen.

Week 2, Monday

Make Me a Cake

Bible Reading

But after a while the wadi dried up, because there was no rain in the land. Then the word of the Lord came to him, saying, "Go now to Zarephath, which belongs to Sidon, and live there; for I have commanded a widow there to feed you." So he set out and went to Zarephath. When he came to the gate of the town, a widow was there gathering sticks; he called to her and said, "Bring me a little water in a vessel, so that I may drink." As she was going to bring it, he called to her and said, "Bring me a morsel of bread in your hand." But she said, "As the Lord your God lives, I have nothing baked, only a handful of meal in a jar, and a little oil in a jug; I am now gathering a couple of sticks, so that I may go home and prepare it for myself and my son, that we may eat it, and die." Elijah said to her, "Do not be afraid; go and do as you have said; but first make me a little cake of it and bring it to me, and afterwards make something for yourself and your son. For thus says the Lord the God of Israel: The jar of meal will not be emptied and the jug of oil will not fail until the day that the Lord sends rain on the earth." She went and did as Elijah said, so that she as well as he and her household ate for many days. The jar of meal was not emptied, neither did the jug of oil fail, according to the word of the Lord that he spoke by Elijah.

1 Kings 17:7-16

The Voice of Salome

My name is Salome. I am the mother of a boy who died but was revived and rescued from death by the prophet Elijah.

Our land had been struck by a heavy drought. It had not rained for years. All the crops had failed, and food was running short. In fact, I had enough flour and oil left to bake just one more meal for my son and myself – before starvation and death would be our fate.

Into our village came a man – old and unkempt, but with a kind face and an air of authority about him. He approached us as we slowly gathered wood to build our final fire.

"Please," he said, "can you make me a cake?"

I almost laughed in his face. "We have nothing!" I explained, and I spelt out our predicament to him.

"I have come from God," he told us. "He has promised that if you help me, the little flour and oil you have will never run dry. Trust in the God of your ancestors and deliverance will be yours."

I made a cake for the man of God and, true to his word, the flour and oil we had never ran out. The man stayed with us for months and months, until the rains came and our fields were once again ready for the harvest.

Time passed, but with every passing day my son grew weaker. I watched as he deteriorated in front of my eyes. I cried out to God – the God who had saved us from certain death – could he now restore my son's health?

But death came.

I didn't know what to do with myself. I beat my chest and wept until my eyes had no more tears left. *Where was God now?*

Then, when all hope seemed lost, Elijah returned.

I pleaded with him. "I helped you. Now, could you help me and restore my son?"

It was a bold request, but the prophet didn't flinch. Instead, he knelt and prayed. Then he took my son in his arms and breathed over him.

To my amazement, my son opened his eyes! He was alive!

From then on, I followed Elijah's 'career' with interest. There was, for example, the 'battle of the barbecues', as I call it, against the supporters of a god named Baal. There, the challenge to light a fire with a lightning bolt was laid down; Elijah's God not only did that but he managed to light a pile of wood that had been soaked in water to show his power…

Then there was the time Elijah fled the wrath of the queen, who hunted him down whilst he hid in a cave. There God came to him. There was a great wind, a fire and an earthquake, and yet Elijah realised that

God was not in any of these. Rather, as they passed, Elijah heard God in the still small voice of calm.

Pause for Thought

- Have you ever been asked to give up what little you have to help someone else? Might God be asking you to do that in this season?
- Has God ever demonstrated healing in your life or in people you know? Thank him for that now.
- Do you find stillness helpful or is this something you shy away from, and why?

Action

Set aside some time to sit still for five minutes and listen for God's still voice of calm. Perhaps you could set an alarm on your phone so that you don't need to check how much time has passed. Ask yourself what God might be saying to you in this time and space.

Prayer

God of Elijah, who restored the dead child to life again,
come and help me to know your still voice of calm.
Amidst the busyness of my life,
help me to find space for you,
so that you can show me what you would have me do.
Amen.

WEEK 2, TUESDAY

The Servant's Song

Bible Reading

In the year that King Uzziah died, I saw the Lord sitting on a throne, high and lofty; and the hem of his robe filled the temple. Seraphs were in attendance above him; each had six wings: with two they covered their faces, and with two they covered their feet, and with two they flew. Then one of the seraphs flew to me, holding a live coal that had been taken from the altar with a pair of tongs. The seraph touched my mouth with it and said: "Now that this has touched your lips, your guilt has departed and your sin is blotted out." Then I heard the voice of the Lord saying, "Whom shall I send, and who will go for us?" And I said, "Here am I; send me!"

Isaiah 6:1,2,6-8

If you have time, you could read more of Isaiah's story in Isaiah 9, 11, 40, 42, 43, 50 and 53.

The Voice of Isaiah

It all began in the year that King Uzziah died. I was a young man then, but now I am old and nearing the end of my life. However, before I 'go to glory' and join my God, I wanted to share the pathway of my life and the pictures God gave me, so that others might draw strength and trust from my story.

It started with a dream – a vision, really, but I wasn't hallucinating. I saw myself standing in the courts of God, in the throne room of the Almighty. Suddenly, I was not alone. I was surrounded by creatures, the like of which I had never seen before, or since. Each one had six wings and they flew all around me.

I covered my eyes because I felt so vulnerable. I was afraid that I would die if I saw God. I knew I was not worthy to be the company of such angelic beings, yet there I was. Then one of the creatures touched my lips with a burning coal and I heard the voice of God speak to me.

"Whom shall I send and who will go for us?"

I was overrun by emotion, swept up in the very moment. So before I even really knew what I was doing, I was putting up my hand. I hadn't thought it through, hadn't undertaken a risk assessment. I hadn't even consulted my loved ones.

"I'll go," I said. "Send me!"

And send me he did. He sent me to "an unclean people" with "unclear lips". He sent me to tell them to repent and turn back to him. There was no going back – no pretending it had all been just a dream. This was my new reality: *I was a prophet of God.*

Years passed, and over time God's message changed: destruction was in the past, repentance was the order of the day, and hope was at hand – the hope of a child to be born, a son to be given who would be called "wonderful, counsellor, mighty God, everlasting father and prince of peace". He would come from the line and the throne of David, and he would establish a kingdom built on justice and peace. A people who were 'walking in darkness' would see the light dawn.

However, the child that was born would not remain a child, of course. He would grow and become a man – a man who would be a servant even to servants and who would lay down his life for his friends. He would redefine all things. He would be like a shepherd for scattered sheep. He would also be treated badly – his beard would be pulled, he would be mocked and he would be whipped on the back by his aggressors. Ultimately, he would take upon his shoulders the sins of the world. He would suffer and die alone and in agony.

Nevertheless, this would not be the end. Hope would come again. He would rise up, like an eagle taking flight. He would never grow tired or weak again. The child of hope would come to stay forever. He would make his home among us. He would come and renew his people, and everything would change.

Pause for Thought

- Isaiah agreed to be God's messenger, almost without thinking. Would you be as willing to say those words, "Here I am. Send me."?
- The servant songs[1] are beautiful writings, but what do they mean? Is Isaiah speaking of Christ?
- What does it mean for Christmas if we hold the cross at the centre?

Action

Find an opportunity to serve others. For example, you could prepare a meal for those you love and serve it to them.

Remember that Jesus was the servant of the servants, and knelt and washed his friends' feet.

Prayer

Lord of the manger and of the cross,
    thank you that you are with me
    as I prepare to greet you again this year.
Help me to remember that even when you were a baby,
    the cross that lay ahead was always the purpose of your life.
Help me to work with those around me to share your story,
    not just one of a baby born in a stable,
    but of a man who died for our salvation.
Amen.

---

[1] Isaiah chapters 42, 49, 50, 52 and 53

WEEK 2, WEDNESDAY

Walk Humbly With Your God

Bible Reading

Hear what the Lord says: Rise, plead your case before the mountains, and let the hills hear your voice. Hear, you mountains, the controversy of the LORD, and you enduring foundations of the earth; for the LORD has a controversy with his people, and he will contend with Israel.
"O my people, what have I done to you? In what have I wearied you? Answer me! For I brought you up from the land of Egypt, and redeemed you from the house of slavery; and I sent before you Moses, Aaron, and Miriam. O my people, remember now what King Balak of Moab devised, what Balaam son of Beor answered him, and what happened from Shittim to Gilgal, that you may know the saving acts of the Lord."
"With what shall I come before the Lord, and bow myself before God on high? Shall I come before him with burnt offerings, with calves a year old? Will the Lord be pleased with thousands of rams, with ten thousands of rivers of oil? Shall I give my firstborn for my transgression, the fruit of my body for the sin of my soul?"
He has told you, O mortal, what is good; and what does the Lord require of you but to do justice, and to love kindness, and to walk humbly with your God?

Micah 6:1-8

The Voice of Micah

My name is Micah, and I was a prophet during the reigns of three kings of Judah. When God foretold his judgement on the people for their sins, he showed me visions of his vengeance, of mountains melting beneath him and of valleys being split apart – "...like wax before a fire or like rushing waters down a hillside," I was told.

God warned about the wicked – those who wanted status or defrauded people and robbed others of their inheritance. He spoke of false prophets and those that would lead others astray. He rebuked the leaders and the rulers, and those who allowed power to corrupt them. They would be punished, he said. He had a case to bring against his people, the people he had brought out of Egypt, who had been slaves and now had been delivered.

However, amid the warnings and the judgement there was always hope – a promise that he would bring them to the safety and to an abundance of green pastures. In the days to come, the Lord promised a new Temple, built on the mountain of God. Here peace would reign; here all people would learn his ways. Swords would be beaten into gardening tools and spears would become like pruning hooks. In this time and this place, nations would no longer take up arms against other nations, and no-one would train for war. The Lord had a plan and I was to be the messenger, to reveal it to his people.

This was the plan: God would gather the lame, assemble the exiles and turn them once again into a great nation. The Lord would rule, and his people would be saved from their enemies. Out of Bethlehem, the smallest of the tribes of Israel, he would bring a man whose origins stretched back to before the beginning of time. Israel will not be discarded; our hands will be lifted up in triumph and those that follow and obey God will know salvation.

What does God want, and what does he ask of his people? Burnt offerings? Rivers of gold? A firstborn son? *No!* Just this: that we act justly, love mercy and walk humbly with him.

Now I wait for the holy one of God, who will call all to act justly, to value mercy, to love unconditionally, and to walk with him, our comfort and friend.

Pause for Thought

- What does it mean for us to act justly, love mercy and walk humbly with God?
- What might that look like in your life?
- Can you call God your friend?

Action

We receive so many requests from charities for support that we easily grow deaf to the cries, popping request letters straight into the bin. The next time you receive one, stop and read it through carefully. Ask yourself, how God would view justice in the situation being described? Can you help to bring a measure of justice in a practical way?

Prayer

God of mercy and forgiveness,
    help me to learn what it really means
    to act justly, love mercy and walk humbly with you.
Help me to show your love and your mercy
    to all those with whom I have contact today.
May I demonstrate your justice towards all I meet.
In your name.
Amen.

WEEK 2, THURSDAY

It Swallowed Me Whole

Bible Reading

Now the word of the Lord came to Jonah son of Amittai, saying, "Go at once to Nineveh, that great city, and cry out against it; for their wickedness has come up before me." But Jonah set out to flee to Tarshish from the presence of the Lord. He went down to Joppa and found a ship going to Tarshish; so he paid his fare and went on board, to go with them to Tarshish, away from the presence of the Lord. But the Lord hurled a great wind upon the sea, and such a mighty storm came upon the sea that the ship threatened to break up. Then the mariners were afraid, and each cried to his god. They threw the cargo that was in the ship into the sea, to lighten it for them. Jonah, meanwhile, had gone down into the hold of the ship and had lain down, and was fast asleep. The captain came and said to him, "What are you doing sound asleep? Get up, call on your god! Perhaps the god will spare us a thought so that we do not perish." The sailors said to one another, "Come, let us cast lots, so that we may know on whose account this calamity has come upon us." So they cast lots, and the lot fell on Jonah. Then they said to him, "What shall we do to you, that the sea may quiet down for us?" For the sea was growing more and more tempestuous. He said to them, "Pick me up and throw me into the sea; then the sea will quiet down for you; for I know it is because of me that this great storm has come upon you." So they picked Jonah up and threw him into the sea; and the sea ceased from its raging. Then the men feared the Lord even more, and they offered a sacrifice to the Lord and made vows. But the

Lord provided a large fish to swallow up Jonah; and Jonah was in the belly of the fish three days and three nights.

Jonah 1:1-7,11-12,15-17

The Voice of Jonah

I am not a prophet nor a 'man of God'. When I heard God calling out to me, I ran in the opposite direction! My name is Jonah, and my story is very well known. I was the one who was swallowed whole by a giant fish.

I was minding my own business one afternoon, when a messenger of God showed up with a job for me. "God wants you to go to the city of Nineveh," I was told, "and get the people there to repent and turn back to him." *What a joke!*

"Why do you not go yourself?" I challenged him. "I'll tell you why: because Nineveh is a dark and horrible place. No one there cares about God, and if I would rock up there with a message like this, I would certainly not come out alive. If God wants someone to go to Nineveh, he can find someone else. You go!"

I was clear on that. So clear, in fact, that I boarded a boat bound for a port on the other side of the known world. There I found a quiet space below deck and fell asleep. Becoming an agent for God was the *last* item on my agenda right now – if it was on my agenda at all...

My escape had not gone unnoticed. Before too long, the boat began to pitch in the growing swell of waves. The wind howled, and the rain began to lash upon the wooden decks.

I was woken by men in panic. "Get up!" I was told. "Start praying. Maybe your God can save us from certain death at the hands of this storm."

I knew the weather conditions were probably down to me. I had angered God, and I decided that the only way out was for me to throw myself on his mercy. I ordered the sailors to cast me overboard and I waited on his grace.

Indeed, the winds stilled and the waves hushed, and suddenly I was face to face with a massive fish. It opened its mouth and swallowed me whole. I expected to die...

Yet, there I lay, dishevelled but alive, in the gut of a fish, among decomposing food, muscle and bone. *For three days.* The smell was horrendous and I often choked for air, but one thing is for certain: it concentrated my mind! My prayer there was heartfelt; I willingly recommitted myself to my God and to his service.

Eventually, the fish spat me out.

Then, once again, God called. This time, there was no more running. I was Nineveh-bound.

I walked through the city, where evil was displayed on every corner. I shared my message and waited for the fallout of God's judgement – but it didn't come. The people repented, offered prayers, put on sackcloth and ashes (a sign of deep sadness), fasted and gave themselves to God. I was amazed, but my surprise changed to anger as God announced his forgiveness.

I demonstrated my frustration, but God was unfazed by my anger. In his mercy, he again welcomed me into his presence.

Pause for Thought

- Jonah was called by God but chose to run away. Has God called you to do something that you are running away from?
- Jonah spent three days inside the big fish, which helped him focus on God. What would help you to focus your life on God more?
- Jonah was angry at God's forgiveness. Have you ever experienced God's forgiveness? Do you need to ask for his forgiveness today?

Action

The next time you see a tablet dissolving in water and disappearing, spend a moment to think about how God forgives our sins and allows us to start again.

Prayer

God of the big fish,
    help me to focus on you and
    to put my trust in your love, mercy and forgiveness.
Help me to forgive those around me,
    just as I am forgiven by you.

I recommit myself to you,
    to be the child of God you are calling me to be,
    in the name of Jesus Christ.
Amen.

WEEK 2, FRIDAY

For Such a Time as This

Bible Reading

Hathach went out to Mordecai in the open square of the city in front of the king's gate, and Mordecai told him all that had happened to him, and the exact sum of money that Haman had promised to pay into the king's treasuries for the destruction of the Jews. Mordecai also gave him a copy of the written decree issued in Susa for their destruction, that he might show it to Esther, explain it to her, and charge her to go to the king to make supplication to him and entreat him for her people. Hathach went and told Esther what Mordecai had said. Then Esther spoke to Hathach and gave him a message for Mordecai, saying, "All the king's servants and the people of the king's provinces know that if any man or woman goes to the king inside the inner court without being called, there is but one law – all alike are to be put to death. Only if the king holds out the golden scepter to someone, may that person live. I myself have not been called to come in to the king for thirty days." When they told Mordecai what Esther had said, Mordecai told them to reply to Esther, "Do not think that in the king's palace you will escape any more than all the other Jews. For if you keep silence at such a time as this, relief and deliverance will rise for the Jews from another quarter, but you and your father's family will perish. Who knows? Perhaps you have come to royal dignity for just such a time as this."

Esther 4:6-14

If you have time, you could read the whole story in Esther 1-4.

The Voice of Esther

My name is Esther. I am a Jew and I am very proud of the heritage I hold. I did not have a very good start in life as I was an orphan. However, I was raised by a very kind uncle who shared his faith and confidence in our God with me. He told me stories from his childhood, of how the people of Israel, my people, were chosen and blessed by God.

I grew into a wise and beautiful young woman who, it turned out, had also been chosen by God. You could say I was 'named and claimed'! For such a time as this! Let me share my story…

My uncle and I lived in a small house, not far from the king's palace, and it was not long before the king's advisors noticed me. When the king was looking for a wife, I made it to the top of the list and, despite the competition, I soon become queen of the Persian empire.

Not long after this, one of the king's men became hostile towards the Jewish people: treated them badly; exploited them and discriminated against them. He made life difficult for them and eventually sought to kill and destroy all who bore the name of 'Jew'.

My uncle came to me. "You have the king's ear," he said. "You are his wife. Talk to him on behalf of your people. Stand up and be counted as one of us."

However, *no one* approached the king; it was against all the rules of court. You almost needed an invitation. It was the same even for me. Yet, my people's distress disturbed me, so I prayed for guidance, strength and courage.

God's assurance came. He told me that I was where I was for "such a time as this". He had placed me in this position at this point in history so that I could help his people.

I was afraid going to the king. It came with its own risks; if he so chose, it would be *my* death that would come. Still, I kept in mind that people would die if I did not take this step – thousands of them, citizens of God's kingdom; slaughtered, just because of their race and faith in God. I had a job to do, I had no choice, so trembling I approached the throne.

To my amazement, the king listened to me. He put an end to the plan to kill all the Jews and punished his corrupt advisor instead. My God had filled me with his courage and placed me here… for such a time as this.

Pause for Thought

- Do you feel afraid and in need of God's strength and courage at this time? If so, talk to him about this in prayer.
- Do you believe, like Esther, that God has placed you where you are "for such a time as this"? How can you respond to that?
- Esther went to the king, knowing she was taking her life in her hands for the good of others. What might God be asking you to do today for the good of others?

Action

The next time you see someone wearing a medal, whether for sports achievement, military service or outstanding contribution to society, think for a moment about the courage and determination they would have needed in order to gain that medal. Then think about the courage that God offers to give you today. In what situations do you need his courage?

Prayer

God of Esther, who positioned her for "such a time as this",
help me to be ready to fulfil my role today.
Grant me the strength and courage that you gave to Esther
so that I will be brave enough to face
whatever you have planned for me.
Amen.

WEEK 2, SATURDAY

The Master Builder

Bible Reading

The words of Nehemiah son of Hacaliah. In the month of Chislev, in the twentieth year, while I was in Susa the capital, one of my brothers, Hanani, came with certain men from Judah; and I asked them about the Jews that survived, those who had escaped the captivity, and about Jerusalem. They replied, "The survivors there in the province who escaped captivity are in great trouble and shame; the wall of Jerusalem is broken down, and its gates have been destroyed by fire." When I heard these words I sat down and wept, and mourned for days, fasting and praying before the God of heaven. I said, "O Lord God of heaven, the great and awesome God who keeps covenant and steadfast love with those who love him and keep his commandments; let your ear be attentive and your eyes open to hear the prayer of your servant that I now pray before you day and night for your servants, the people of Israel, confessing the sins of the people of Israel, which we have sinned against you. Both I and my family have sinned. We have offended you deeply, failing to keep the commandments, the statutes, and the ordinances that you commanded your servant Moses.

Nehemiah 1:1-7

The Voice of Nehemiah

My name is Nehemiah and I am a wine merchant by trade. Although unqualified, I became a high official within the Persian court and was enlisted by God as a master builder. On paper I should never have got the job, but before I knew it I was commissioned to rebuild the walls of Jerusalem.

Years had passed since God's ungrateful and disobedient people had been scattered to the four ends of the earth. Back then, Jerusalem was destroyed and all hope seemed to be lost. Those believers who were not killed were bound and marched out of the city, banished from their homes, from the Temple and seemingly from God. The God of Israel was still faithful to them though, which is why he now sent me to rebuild not only the walls of Jerusalem, but also his covenant relationship with the people.

I went to see for myself: the walls were a mound of rubble, the gates were cinders and the returning exiles were in a bad way. So I cried, fasted and prayed earnestly before God, confessing my sins and the sins of my ancestors. I even dared to remind the Almighty of a promise once made: that he would gather the remnant and rebuild his Temple.

Under the cover of darkness, the building began, but so did the moaning and complaining. The people were hungry, afraid and unsure of God's provision. I was angry that they could not, or would not, put their trust in him.

I reminded them of their history, beginning with Abraham and Moses, recalling their deliverance from slavery, and more; still, they had gone their own way, chosen selfishness over kindness, and death over life.

We kept on building. Mile by mile, stone by stone, the walls were rebuilt, the doors were re-hung and the gates of the city were secured again.

As the walls grew strong, so did the pressure from our enemies; they pressed us harder and those inside the walls wavered again. Nevertheless, God was as strong as his word; I posted guards as instructed and when the trumpet sounded, he fought on our behalf.

A new stage was set. Israel had moved into a fresh phase. Now we waited for God's salvation to be fully revealed – at his time, in his place and on his command.

Pause for Thought

- Nehemiah was asked to do a difficult task for which he was not really equipped. Again and again, God chooses people that might not at first glance seem appropriate. Has God asked you to do something that is outside of your comfort zone or skillset? What is your response?

- Nehemiah was angry with the people for not trusting God. Have there been times in your life when you have not trusted him? How about now – will you recommit your heart to put your trust in him again?
- The people found that pressure from their enemies grew as they obeyed God. Have you started out on something God put in your heart, but then stopped because of difficult circumstances or opposition from others? If so, will you choose to begin to 'rebuild the walls', to complete what God has started through you?

Action

The next time you find yourself playing with a child, building with blocks or Lego, think about Nehemiah rebuilding the walls of the city but also rebuilding the people's broken relationship with God. Think about how Jesus fully repaired this relationship and what it means to you. If appropriate, perhaps you could share the story of Nehemiah with the child you are playing with?

Prayer

God of relationship,
help me to work on my relationship with you
so that I will be better equipped to build significant relationships with others.
Where there is relationship breakdown,
help me to forgive and rebuild
by leaning on, and trusting in, you.
Amen.

The Hope Realised

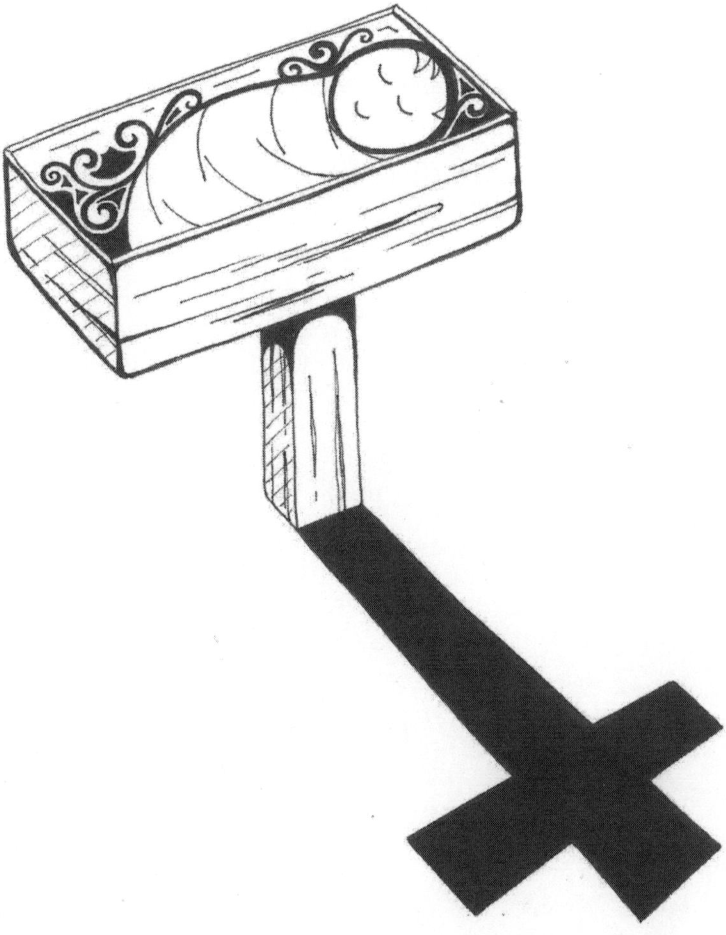

A Recipe for Advent

Hold hope in your hand.
Hold expectation in the other.
Mix it with a dose of uncertainty,
And stir well.
Add a bucketload of willingness,
The need to wait on God,
With a double helping of apprehension
As to what God might ask of you next.
Add openness, time, space and silence to the mixture.
Stir well again.
Place everything –
Heart,
Mind,
Soul
Strength –
Into a heat-proof vessel, then wait.
Cook till golden brown and serve still warm,
Ready to offer your very life to God.

3RD SUNDAY OF ADVENT

Comfort My People

Bible Reading

Now a certain man was ill, Lazarus of Bethany, the village of Mary and her sister Martha. ... When Jesus arrived, he found that Lazarus had already been in the tomb four days. Now Bethany was near Jerusalem, some two miles way, and many of the Jews had come to Martha and Mary to console them about their brother. When Martha heard that Jesus was coming, she went and met him, while Mary stayed at home. Martha said to Jesus, "Lord, if you had been here, my brother would not have died. But even now I know that God will give you whatever you ask of him." Jesus said to her, "Your brother will rise again." Martha said to him, "I know that he will rise again in the resurrection on the last day." Jesus said to her, "I am the resurrection and the life. Those who believe in me, even though they die, will live, and everyone who lives and believes in me will never die. Do you believe this?" She said to him, "Yes, Lord, I believe that you are the Messiah, the Son of God, the one coming into the world."

John 11:1,17-27

The Voice of Joy

Jesus says:

"I am the voice of joy – as foretold in the scriptures. The prophets of ages past spoke of me as they tried to comfort God's people. The Father, the Holy Spirit and I had created them and led them out of slavery, but they had turned away and chosen to follow their own paths. The prophets erected signposts to guide them. They called for repentance. But the people continued to walk blindly.

"Therefore, my father sent me – his only son. I lived among the people and demonstrated love first-hand. I brought comfort and joy, I brought healing and wholeness, and I brought the offer of eternal life. I drew many to myself, offering life, hope and comfort in the midst of death, grief and pain.

"One day, I heard that a friend of mine, Lazarus, was ill. I had healed many, so why not one more? – and one whom I loved dearly, at that. Yet I was slow to respond, and people wondered why. 'Comfort, comfort my people,' an ancient prophet had cried, but how could I offer comfort if I did not understand the pain of grief? I could have visited Lazarus and his sisters in his last days, seen him while he was still alive; I could have prayed for him in his final moments. I didn't though. I chose to wait, to allow my friend to die. I chose to taste suffering and grief just like any other human being. I too felt the emptiness of loss; I too now understood what it meant to be human, as I stood with my friends and wept.

"Later we gathered at the graveside. I spoke words of comfort to Lazarus' sisters, and they did the same for me. Yet, I had my father's ear, and I had the gift of eternal life, so I called, shouted aloud, 'COME OUT! WAKE UP!' – and he did! Lazarus arose and began to breathe and live again. My friend was back from the dead, back in the arms of those who loved him, back to tell the tale.

"I embraced him, despite the bandages that confined him and the smell that lingered heavy in the air. In love I held him, offering him the same comfort that had been offered to me only days before.

"I healed those that needed healing. When I spoke, the lame walked, the blind gained sight, lepers where cleansed and demons where sent packing. The plan was always to point the way to God, to demonstrate his forgiveness and share his love.

"'Comfort, comfort my people,' came the shout, and I did. So, let the words of comfort ring out today, and allow me to offer that same comfort to you and those around you."

Pause for Thought

- Why do you think Jesus did not go to see his friend when he first heard he was ill?
- Have you ever experienced the comfort that Jesus offers?
- How can we begin to offer Jesus' comfort to those around us?

Action

What do you find comforting – an item that brings significant memories, a hug from a friend, a warm fire on a winter's day, a cosy blanket to wrap up in?

Now think, how can you offer somebody else comfort who really needs it? Then plan to do it – allow Jesus to comfort someone through your actions today.

Prayer

God of comfort,
help me to look to you for my comfort,
to become aware of your presence and hear your words.
Show me how to offer your comfort to those around me,
to bring hope to those who feel trapped in suffering and
healing to those who are hurting.
Amen.

Week 3, Monday

A God-incidence

Bible Reading

In the days of King Herod of Judea, there was a priest named Zechariah, who belonged to the priestly order of Abijah. His wife was a descendant of Aaron, and her name was Elizabeth. Both of them were righteous before God, living blamelessly according to all the commandments and regulations of the Lord. But they had no children, because Elizabeth was barren, and both were getting on in years. Once when he was serving as priest before God and his section was on duty, he was chosen by lot, according to the custom of the priesthood, to enter the sanctuary of the Lord and offer incense. Now at the time of the incense offering, the whole assembly of the people was praying outside. Then there appeared to him an angel of the Lord, standing at the right side of the altar of incense. When Zechariah saw him, he was terrified; and fear overwhelmed him. But the angel said to him, "Do not be afraid, Zechariah, for your prayer has been heard. Your wife Elizabeth will bear you a son, and you will name him John. You will have joy and gladness, and many will rejoice at his birth, for he will be great in the sight of the Lord. He must never drink wine or strong drink; even before his birth he will be filled with the Holy Spirit. He will turn many of the people of Israel to the Lord their God. With the spirit and power of Elijah he will go before him, to turn the hearts of parents to their children, and the disobedient to the wisdom of the righteous, to make ready a people prepared for the Lord." Zechariah said to the angel, "How will I know that this is so? For I am an old man, and my wife is getting on in years." The angel replied, "I am Gabriel. I stand in the presence of God, and I have been sent to speak to you and to bring you this good news."

Luke 1:5-19

The Voice of Zechariah

I asked myself time and time again, when does coincidence become God-incidence? How many bits of the puzzle need to come together before a person acknowledges God's controlling and powerful hand? Is it something you just take for granted or, like me, do you need some convincing? Let me tell you my story.

My name is Zechariah, and I am a priest, a servant of the Temple and of the God of Israel. One year, when King Herod was on the throne of Judea, it became the turn of my branch of the priestly orders to be on Temple duty. According to our customs, all the names of the priests are put into a hat, and mine was chosen at random. I would have the privilege of burning the sacrificial incense for God. Was that luck? A coincidence? Or had God planned it that way?

I went inside the holy part of the Temple, the part reserved only for the priests. Everyone else stayed outside and prayed. I admit, my mind was not completely focused on the task. I was thinking about my wife Elizabeth, and how we were old and childless and desperate for an heir.

Was it a coincidence that these thoughts were on my mind, rather than being focused on God, when suddenly, through the fog of incense, an angel appeared, standing at the side of the altar?

I was terrified, as you can imagine, and I fell to my knees, hiding my head in my hands.

"Do not be afraid, Zechariah," came the kind and gentle voice.

The angel knew my name! This was clearly no coincidence; surely this had to be of God. He told me that my prayers had been answered; that Elizabeth would bear a son – a son who would take the name of John, and who would turn the hearts of the people back to God. He would be filled with the Holy Spirit even before his birth, and he would make straight (prepare) the way for the coming Messiah.

It is strange – when you are focused on a problem, it gets out of proportion and you miss what God is up to. All these 'coincidences' and I still didn't recognise the plan and power of God. "How can this be?" I found myself asking the angel. "My wife is unable to have children, and we are both old." It seems crazy that I replied this way, now that I think about it.

But the angel spoke with sincerity. "I am Gabriel," he explained. "I stand in the presence of God, and he has sent me to you to share this good news. Now, because you did not believe my words, you will be silent until these events come to pass."

Then he disappeared.

I emerged, visibly shaken, to pronounce the blessing on the people, but when I opened my mouth to speak, nothing came out. It was just as the angel had said.

Furthermore, as Gabriel had announced, a son *was* born to us and we named him John. He grew and indeed became God's messenger – the one who preached repentance and bestowed God's forgiveness on his people. Our son was not a co-incidence at all – definitely a *God-incidence.*

Pause for Thought

- Can you think of a time when you have experienced a 'God-incidence'?
- How willing are you to acknowledge God's leading in your life?
- God wants us to play our part in his big picture. Are you willing to do that? If so, tell him today!

Action

The next time you find yourself working on a jigsaw puzzle, pause for a moment and think about how you fit into God's big picture. What is the 'shape' he has made you? Thank him for the part he has given you to play.

Prayer

God of surprises,
help me to recognise your presence in all situations
and to acknowledge when you are intervening in my life.

Help me to identify the shape that you have made me,
    fitting into your big picture,
    and to choose to be that shape.
Amen.

WEEK 3, TUESDAY

Another Twitch of the Curtain

Bible Reading

Mary said to the angel, "How can this be, since I am a virgin?" The angel said to her, "The Holy Spirit will come upon you, and the power of the Most High will overshadow you; therefore the child to be born will be holy; he will be called Son of God. And now, your relative Elizabeth in her old age has also conceived a son; and this is the sixth month for her who was said to be barren. For nothing will be impossible with God." Then Mary said, "Here am I, the servant of the Lord; let it be with me according to your word." Then the angel departed from her.

Luke 1:34-38

And Mary said, "My soul magnifies the Lord, and my spirit rejoices in God my Saviour, for he has looked with favour on the lowliness of his servant. Surely, from now on all generations will call me blessed; for the Mighty One has done great things for me, and holy is his name. His mercy is for those who fear him from generation to generation."

Luke 1:46-50

The Voice of Mary

There goes another one, another twitch of another curtain. The gossip-mongers are out in force and I am the talk of the town.

My name is Mary – well, that is the term that *polite* people use when speaking of me; I don't want to mention what the less polite ones call me.

I guess I don't blame them. After all, the evidence is damning: a young, unmarried girl, heavily pregnant; spouting some unrealistic waffle about an angel, conception through the Holy Spirit and giving birth to God's only son. Whatever next!

However, every word of it is true. Let me tell you my story.

I am a single girl from Nazareth, engaged to an older, wiser man by the name of Joseph. My parents chose him for me, but he is a good man with a good job and a steady income and, to be honest, I am absolutely in love with him!

One day, still waiting for the wedding, I was doing the daily round of jobs, when the house became ablaze with light. There in front of me stood an angel in a shining white robe.

"Do not be afraid," he said. "I am Gabriel and I bring you news of great joy. You are chosen by God; you will carry and give birth to his son, Jesus, the Messiah, who will redeem his people."

I was a God-fearing young woman, so despite my fear and disbelief, I questioned him. "How can this be?" I asked.

"The Spirit of God will touch you, and a child will be conceived. He will reign over the people of God, and his kingdom will have no end."

What was I to say? What was I to do? This was all completely insane! I was not of royal blood; I was just a normal girl. Surely there had been a mix-up, a case of mistaken identity? Yet the angel seemed convinced; his mission strategy was clear: sign up the girl and God will do the rest.

My first instinct was to run, but I calmed myself and began to accept the part I would play in God's ongoing story. "I am the servant of my God," I said, resigning myself to all that was to come: the shame, the whispers, the dagger-looks, the disappointment in Joseph's eyes.

A backstreet wedding awaits me now, and a long and tiring journey to Bethlehem, as well as the pain of childbirth and all that will follow. My heart is already so full of love for a child that is only partly mine – a child who will grow into a man and, I believe, live and die to rebuild the broken relationship between us and God.

Pause for Thought

- Mary was asked to bear God's son. Imagine you were asked the same; how might you react?
- Just as Mary was chosen by God, the Bible teaches that we are chosen too. What does that mean to you?

- At the beginning of Jesus' life, the curtains in the houses twitched their disapproval, but in the end, the Temple curtain was literally ripped from top to bottom to make God accessible to all. Can you entrust your own difficult circumstances to God today, to turn around for good?

Action

Look up Amnesty International *(www.amnesty.org.uk)*. Read about their work and think about those in the world today who are judged or rejected. Consider how you could help to make a difference. Maybe you could write a letter to a political prisoner, or to an MP, about a specific issue.

Prayer

God of justice, who called Mary to carry your son
    and bear the brunt of discrimination and gossip,
    help me to look to you for my sense of security and purpose,
    and to find the peace in you that Mary found.
Help me to respond to your call in the way she did,
    by offering myself completely to you.
Please grant me the grace for all you call me to do,
    just as you did with her.
Amen.

WEEK 3, WEDNESDAY

Chip off the Old Block

Bible Reading

Now the birth of Jesus the Messiah took place in this way. When his mother Mary had been engaged to Joseph, but before they lived together, she was found to be with child from the Holy Spirit. Her husband Joseph, being a righteous man and unwilling to expose her to public disgrace, planned to dismiss her quietly. But just when he had resolved to do this, an angel of the Lord appeared to him in a dream and said, "Joseph, son of David, do not be afraid to take Mary as your wife, for the child conceived in her is from the Holy Spirit. She will bear a son, and you are to name him Jesus, for he will save his people from their sins." All this took place to fulfil what had been spoken by the Lord through the prophet: "Look, the virgin shall conceive and bear a son, and they shall name him Emmanuel," which means, "God is with us." When Joseph awoke from sleep, he did as the angel of the Lord commanded him; he took her as his wife, but had no marital relations with her until she had borne a son; and he named him Jesus.

Matthew 1:18-25

Voice of Joseph

My name is Joseph, and I discovered first-hand that the best-laid plans of man or beast do not always sit well with the plans of God.

I was a respectable carpenter. I had a good business, and I was not short of money either. I came from good stock, and I was engaged to Mary, a good and decent woman, young and beautiful; she would make me a good wife and bear me a son to carry on the family name. My life was all mapped out – or so I thought...

She stood in the doorway, her eyes filled with tears. What was wrong? What secret was she hiding? Was she ill? Had someone died? *What was it?*

Then she spoke, and as she unburdened herself, my concern turned to violent anger. "Joseph," she said, "I'm going to have a baby."

In rage, I throw my cup against the wall. I wanted to strike her, but my honour would not allow me. Instead, I ushered her towards the door. *What did she mean, she was going to have a baby?*

I loved her and respected her, but this was just too much. She had brought shame upon me and my family, and so she would have to go. I did not want to embarrass her or leave her with nothing, so despite my anger, I prayed that God would show me a kind way to call off the wedding.

I sank into a corner of my workshop, tears rolling down my face. How had it come to this? What a way for it all to end!

Then suddenly, through my tears, I saw a bright light and I was no longer alone. "Joseph," came a voice, "do not be afraid."

It was a bit late for that, wasn't it? I was terrified!

"I am Gabriel, and God has sent me to you. Mary, your fiancée, is pregnant and is going to bear God's son. Take her to yourself, marry her and call her your own. The God of your ancestors has spoken."

Sweat ran down my forehead like a river. Mary had told me the truth.

The angel disappeared as quickly as he had come, leaving me alone again. My anger had gone, I was strangely content, and I knew exactly what I had to do.

I went, took Mary as my wife, and raised God's son as my own. I taught him the skills of a carpenter. In that, at least, he was truly 'a chip off the old block'.

Pause for Thought

- How do you think Joseph must have felt when he heard Mary's news?
- Have you ever felt betrayed? How did you react?
- Could Joseph really think of Jesus as a chip off the old block?

Action

Do you have an angel at the top of your Christmas tree? The next time you see an angel decoration, or a picture of an angel on a Christmas card, stop and remember how Mary and Joseph received messages from God through angels. Ask God in your heart what he wants to say to you today.

Prayer

God of Joseph,
  who asked him to be a human father to your divine son,
  draw me closer to you today and fill me with your Spirit.
Help me to walk alongside those who have been betrayed
  or who are treated unfairly.
In the name of Christ, I pray.
Amen.

WEEK 3, THURSDAY

My Child Danced Inside Me

Bible Reading

In those days Mary set out and went with haste to a Judean town in the hill country, where she entered the house of Zechariah and greeted Elizabeth. When Elizabeth heard Mary's greeting, the child leaped in her womb. And Elizabeth was filled with the Holy Spirit and exclaimed with a loud cry, "Blessed are you among women, and blessed is the fruit of your womb. And why has this happened to me, that the mother of my Lord comes to me? For as soon as I heard the sound of your greeting, the child in my womb leaped for joy. And blessed is she who believed that there would be a fulfilment of what was spoken to her by the Lord."

Luke 1:39-45

The Voice of Elizabeth

I watched as they played together as children – laughing, joking and enjoying life. Yet, I was told time and time again that our joy would not last forever; one day both Jesus' mother and I would know true sorrow, if I lived long enough to see it.

I am old now, but I was already old when all this begun – ageing, apparently unable to have children and almost at the stage of giving up on life altogether. Yet God had other ideas; he had a plan, and Zechariah and I were part of it.

An angel came and explained to my husband that my infertile womb would soon 'bear fruit' and we would have a son. (Not that he was able to tell me any of this at the time, as he had been struck dumb by God due to his unbelief.) The child would be a herald of God and we were to give him the name John.

About six months into my pregnancy, we had a visit from a cousin of mine. We had a surprising amount in common: she too had become pregnant and she too had been spoken to by an angel; she too was going to have a son – one who would redeem the nation in his later life.

We had been told that John, our son, would be full of the Holy Spirit even before his birth. It wasn't till Mary arrived, however, that I began to understand the meaning of this prophecy. As she walked slowly up our path, the child inside me began to leap and dance, as he and I somehow realised that we were in the presence of greatness.

In our country the custom is for young people to respect their elders and seek to serve where it is appropriate. On this occasion, however, I bowed low and offered myself to Mary's service, despite my age and my grey hair. She was a girl who was willing to come under public scrutiny, to have people talking about her behind her back, to be spat on in the street and subjected to the cruel laws that awaited unmarried mothers. Indeed, she was willing to put her life on hold in order to give birth to God's son and to undergo everything that would come with that.

She had to weigh up what her "yes" would mean – to her and to her family – just as I had to. *Our* son would be the forerunner, the one who would set out all that was to come; who would dig up the ground in people's hearts, make paths straight and prepare the way for the coming Messiah.

While Mary stayed with us, our unborn children bonded. Their mothers sewed and conversed, creating more than mere clothes and blankets, as we prepared for the future and the roles we and our offspring would play. Together we began to realise that our lives would not be easy. We placed our hands in one another's, understanding what a terrible burden it was to be chosen by God. Tears flowed freely, God's Spirit was with us and our hearts gradually began to beat in time with the divine.

Pause for Thought

- John was said to be filled with the Holy Spirit before he was born. What do you think that means? Have you been filled with the same Spirit?
- Elizabeth and Mary spoke of how their lives might be. What does/would your life look like with Christ truly at the forefront?

- The women shed tears as they thought about the burden of being chosen by God. Do you feel a similar burden? What is your response to this?

Action

The next time you spend some time with a parent expecting a child, ask whether you can take a moment to pray for the unborn child. If you are given permission, bless the child, thank God for his perfect design being put into place, and pray that the child will grow in their relationship with him.

Prayer

God of new birth,
I pray for those I know who are expecting children.
    Protect these unborn infants and bring them to a place of knowing Jesus as Lord and Saviour.
I pray for those I know who have lost children.
    Comfort them this Christmas;
    may they become aware of your presence and love this season.
Help me to be family-focused,
    and to centre my life around your church family,
    so that together we can show love to our community.
Amen.

Week 4, Friday

We Have a Stable

Bible Reading

In those days a decree went out from Emperor Augustus that all the world should be registered. This was the first registration and was taken while Quirinius was governor of Syria. All went to their own towns to be registered. Joseph also went from the town of Nazareth in Galilee to Judea, to the city of David called Bethlehem, because he was descended from the house and family of David. He went to be registered with Mary, to whom he was engaged and who was expecting a child. While they were there, the time came for her to deliver her child. And she gave birth to her firstborn son and wrapped him in bands of cloth, and laid him in a manger, because there was no place for them in the inn.

Luke 2:1-7

The Voice of the Innkeeper's Wife

Of course, we had all heard the prophecy, but we, like everyone else, never believed that anything important could ever come out of Bethlehem – nothing of any worth, certainly nothing that would impact the whole world.

How wrong we were…

What a weekend it has been! We have been rushed off our feet; hardly had time to draw breath. You see, recently the Emperor in his wisdom (or lack of it) sent everyone back to their home town to be counted. Stupid idea, if you ask me, but I guess no-one is asking me…

Our small, poor, unimportant village has suddenly been overrun with people. Every inn and tavern, including ours, is packed to the rafters. We aren't complaining; it is good for business. We are not going to turn the extra cash down, are we? But it has been manic.

At one point, my husband instructed me to get a sign to tell people we are full. But before I got around to that, there came a knock at the door that changed everything.

Before me stood a young woman – heavily pregnant, with a look of exhaustion etched all over her face. She was aided by an older man and they had a small, weary-looking donkey in tow. They wanted – no, they *needed* – a room, somewhere, *anywhere*, so that the woman could rest her head. Looking at her, it was clear that it wouldn't be long before her child would be greeting the world.

As a woman a of faith, my heart was touched. What could I do to help, to offer some respite from her immediate plight? I explained how sorry I was, that all our rooms were full, but that if she wanted, we had a stable round the back that she could use. It was not five-star by any stretch of the imagination, it wasn't even very clean, but at least it had a roof that didn't leak.

She smiled and silently nodded her approval and her gratitude, and I led the way. We didn't make pleasant small talk; she had bigger things to concentrate on, like going into labour.

I settled her down with some clean hay on which she could rest her head, then told her I would be back with a midwife, some towels and some hot water. "Sit tight!" I instructed them both.

I ran, panic-stricken really. After all, it's not every day that someone is giving birth in your barn! I sent a kitchen hand to call the midwife, then I raided the airing cupboard for towels and fetched the water.

By the time I returned, labour was in full swing. I assisted where I could, wiping the young mother's forehead and offering words of encouragement. Then, after what seemed like an age, although it probably wasn't, I began to see a tiny head followed by the body of a healthy-looking baby boy.

The midwife did what was needed, wrapped the child in a towel and gave him to his mother.

There, in that moment, I somehow knew that I was in the company of someone special. Since then I have strangely sensed that all the prophecies we have heard are beginning to be fulfilled.

Pause for Thought

- Have you seen anyone recently who clearly needs your help? If so, what have you done for them?
- The innkeeper's wife offered what she could. What could you offer during this season to people in need?
- There was a welcome at the stable. Can you offer such a welcome to your friends and neighbours?

Action

Spend a moment to think about whom you might be able to help out – maybe an elderly person, a young child or someone who is struggling in life at this time. What could you do? Take in some shopping, read a story, hold their hand, or simply spend time listening to them and offer a smile.

Prayer

God of welcome,
    you prepared a welcome for your son.
Help me to offer a welcome to all people,
    so that they can experience your unconditional love.
Amen.

WEEK 3, SATURDAY

Send for the Midwife

Bible Reading

The king of Egypt said to the Hebrew midwives, one of whom was named Shiphrah and the other Puah, "When you act as midwives to the Hebrew women, and see them on the birthstool, if it is a boy, kill him; but if it is a girl, she shall live." But the midwives feared God; they did not do as the king of Egypt commanded them, but they let the boys live. So the king of Egypt summoned the midwives and said to them, "Why have you done this, and allowed the boys to live?" The midwives said to Pharaoh, "Because the Hebrew women are not like the Egyptian women; for they are vigorous and give birth before the midwife comes to them." So God dealt well with the midwives; and the people multiplied and became very strong. And because the midwives feared God, he gave them families.

Exodus 1:15-21

The Voice of Martha, a Midwife

It was just another birth – or so I thought. I had delivered so many, I could almost do it with my eyes shut, yet there was something about this one that was so very different. With this child, I followed his life with interest, and I have never done that before, or since. I was there with him as he drew his final breath, just as I was when he drew his first. I was there hiding in the shadows, masked by anonymity. Yet in his dying moments, I vividly remembered his birth…

The town was packed to overflowing. The governor that year had ordered a count of the people – just to make life difficult for everyone, we all secretly thought, although no one dared to voice that at the time.

All the inns and taverns were full, and when a tired, heavily pregnant young woman arrived, she quickly become the talk of the town.

The man she was with pleaded for someone to take pity and find her somewhere, *anywhere,* to lay her weary head. Eventually word came through that a place had been found: a draughty stable out the back of some inn. Not ideal, but better than nothing. The woman was just glad to have somewhere to rest.

Bethlehem was not a quiet, peaceful place in the dead of night. It was still partying; there was still heavy drinking, with more than a few disagreements that got out of hand. The stable wasn't quiet either. But the child inside that young mother-to-be was ready to greet the world, and greet it he did!

I was deep in sleep, not expecting to be woken, when suddenly, someone in panic was pounding on my door. As I rose, my eyes were still sleepy, but that would soon change. I was ushered to the stable and there I helped a mother give birth to her firstborn son. It was with great joy that I handed the tiny bundle to this exhausted, overwhelmed girl. This moment after the birth was always special, but this time it seemed like even the angels in heaven were celebrating. The young mother had tears in her eyes as I handed her the baby boy. Little did any of us know, though, how many more of her tears would be shed as time went on.

I was just about to leave and go back to my bed when the adopted peace was shattered again – not by the child or his mother but by the arrival of some shepherds from the local hillside.

"We have come to see the child," they announced. "Some angels told us about him and we have come to worship him."

Everyone looked at them in horror. Why had they come? No one wanted shepherds around; they were smelly and unkempt, they were the untouchables. But the baby didn't seem to think so, at least; he welcomed their appearance with a giggle.

I know now that I was in the presence of the Messiah, the holy one of God. Aside from the stable and the visitors, the birth itself had seemed routine – I gave the usual words of encouragement, the mother pushed and shoved, screaming in pain. It was the same at every birth. But through this birth, silently and unseen at that time, *everything had changed.*

It was only years later as I stood near the foot of his cross that I understood what had occurred. Somehow God had become man that night, in that stable, and I had been playing my part, taking my place in the story that would shape history.

Pause for Thought

- Martha recognised her part in God's unfolding story. What do you believe your part to be? Whether you know it or not, thank God that he does indeed have a part for you to play in his unfolding plan.
- What is your reaction when you think about God becoming a human?
- Mary experienced childbirth like any other mother through time, but without any of the comfort and security of a hospital. Has following God ever led you to an uncomfortable place? How have you responded to that?

Action

Do you have a set of dominos? Maybe you could teach a child to play. As the spots line up, you could talk about how God fits us into his unfolding story, how each of us has an important part to play.

Prayer

God who came to us in the body of a baby,
    thank you that you are still with me today.
    Fill me again with your hope and peace.
Lord, I pray for those who work in the local hospitals,
    who seek to save lives and comfort the dying.
    Grant them skill in the work they do,
    and your grace to fulfil their part in your unfolding plan.
Help me to show gratitude to those I encounter
    in the healing and caring professions
    for the work they do.
Amen.

4TH SUNDAY OF ADVENT

Peace I Leave You

Bible Reading

"Do not let your hearts be troubled. Believe in God, believe also in me. In my Father's house there are many dwelling places. If it were not so, would I have told you that I go to prepare a place for you? And if I go and prepare a place for you, I will come again and will take you to myself, so that where I am, there you may be also. And you know the way to the place where I am going." Thomas said to him, "Lord, we do not know where you are going. How can we know the way?" Jesus said to him, "I am the way, and the truth, and the life. No one comes to the Father except through me. Peace I leave with you; my peace I give to you. I do not give to you as the world gives. Do not let your hearts be troubled, and do not let them be afraid."

John 14:1-6,27

The Voice of Peace

Jesus says:

"I am the voice of peace – a peace that knows no bounds and goes beyond all understanding. I am the peace that sets people free and binds up broken hearts. I am the voice of peace, given freely to all who wish to receive.

"The prophets of old spoke of my coming and the kingdom I would usher in: a realm where tools of war would be laid down and turned into instruments for peace; a land where peace would have dominion, where wild animals would sleep alongside livestock, and a child would be able to play safely even in the nest of a poisonous snake.

"My birth was far from peaceful: a noisy stable, the arrival of shepherds and a muffled heavenly choir that no one could explain. But as I grew, peace descended upon me, until the time when in the shadow of the cross on which I would be crucified, I offered my peace to my friends and to the world.

"'Don't let your hearts be troubled,' I said. 'Don't worry or be afraid. Put your trust in me and in my father and we will guide you by the hand. I will not always be with you, but I will send you a helper who will walk with you every step of the way. This advocate will strengthen you and be the go-between, straddling heaven and earth.

"'When you go into your room, fall to your knees and pray earnestly to God. When you call on my name, your prayers will be answered according to my will. Seek my father's kingdom first and all things will be given to you. Let me show you the way to heaven, and then everyone who loves me will have a place in paradise. I will go before you and make it ready, so that when I come for you in death, you will be with me forever.'

"Sadly, my friends did not understand; they did not comprehend that I was preparing them for the death that was approaching me – the death that I would face for their good and the good of the world, in order to demonstrate the Father's love. They didn't understand that because of my love for them, I was willing to lay down my life.

"I needed them to know that they would not be left alone and that I offered them my peace and the peace of God. 'I am the voice of peace,' I told them. 'My peace is not the same as the world gives. Mine is everlasting, constant and life-changing. Therefore, do not be afraid and do not worry about anything, for I am with you always – till the end of time.'"

Pause for Thought

- How have you experienced God's peace in your life?
- Have there been times in your life when you have felt afraid? What was the cause of that?
- What word would have changed your fear to a sense of peace? Do you believe that God would have spoken that word to you?

Action

For five minutes or so, try sitting in silence and just become aware that God is close to you and his Spirit is offering you peace. If other thoughts come to mind (e.g. things you need to do later), just write them down and then let them go. Keep your focus on Jesus and receive his peace for today.

Prayer

God of peace,
help me to become more aware of your presence
in the stillness of my heart.
I give you my cares and worries and choose to trust you with them;
now, please fill me again with your love and peace.
I pray for nations currently experiencing war and political turmoil,
that your peace would fill the hearts of the people in those lands
and their leaders.
Amen.

WEEK 4, MONDAY

A Game of Chinese Whispers

Bible Reading

The righteous are delivered from trouble,
and the wicked get into it instead.
With their mouths the godless would destroy their neighbours,
but by knowledge the righteous are delivered.
When it goes well with the righteous, the city rejoices;
and when the wicked perish, there is jubilation.
By the blessing of the upright a city is exalted,
but it is overthrown by the mouth of the wicked.
Whoever belittles another lacks sense,
but an intelligent person remains silent.
A gossip goes about telling secrets,
but one who is trustworthy in spirit keeps a confidence.
Where there is no guidance, a nation falls,
but in an abundance of counsellors there is safety.
To guarantee loans for a stranger brings trouble,
but there is safety in refusing to do so.

Proverbs 11:8-15

The Voice of Dan, a Resident of Bethlehem.

Was it just another game of Chinese whispers, a message passed from person to person – or a tall tale told at a bar, fuelled by alcohol and drugs? Or was there more to it than that?

I had been told the story by a friend... who said he had heard it from a workmate... who had got it from his landlady... who had received it from a shepherd... who apparently had witnessed it first-hand.

It was a saga revolving around a child – born in a stable and laid in an animals' feeding trough. He was a child who somehow commanded respect and offered dignity to all who encountered him, a child whose authority was transcendent without a word being uttered.

The talk was that this child was the one that had been promised, the holy one of God, the Messiah.

This was the story I had been told. So, what was I to do? I needed to see for myself. I felt compelled to take a trip to the stable to see if it was real, to meet the child face to face.

I arrived and found everything just as I had been told. There was his mother cradling him in her arms, his father keeping a vigilant watch – and the boy himself, helpless, vulnerable and yet powerful in innocence. I knew I was in the presence of greatness; every hair on my body seemed to dance. I felt known and loved and valued just by being there.

The young woman smiled at me. "Would you like to hold him?" she asked.

Hold him? Me, a poor and unimportant peasant? *Hold him!* "I'd love to."

I held out my arms and slowly the baby was placed into them. I was overcome with emotion. Tears fell uncontrollably from my eyes. I don't normally show my feelings, but at that moment in time I had no choice. I knew he was no ordinary baby and that I would never be the same again.

Eventually, I pulled myself away, wished the family well and left. Now the ball was in my court. It was my move. What was I going to do – pass on the 'Chinese whisper' or keep it to myself?

My experience had been life-changing. I had arrived on the edge of society, low down in the social rankings; an outcast, unloved and undervalued. Yet I had been welcomed just as I was. I had been handed the saviour of the world, trusted with him, and through that I have been touched by God himself.

So how could I keep quiet? How could I keep the story to myself? For this was a story of transformation, mine and the world's. I knew that I had changed. Now others needed the chance to respond. I no longer wanted to whisper. It was now vital to shout from the rooftops, bellow from the depths of the earth: "The Messiah is here! I have seen him, held him and been made new in him! Hear my story and pass it on!"

Pause for Thought

- The resident of Bethlehem felt that he was unworthy to meet the Christ child. How do you feel about meeting Jesus in prayer and worship?
- He was accepted as he was. How do you respond to God's offer to accept you as you are?
- After his encounter with the Christ, he could no longer keep quiet. Has Jesus changed your life and, if so, whom could you share your story with?

Action

If you have a family or group of friends, perhaps you could share today's meditation and have a game of Chinese Whispers together. Then talk together about how you might share the Good News of Jesus to those you spend time with during this season.

Prayer

God of the poor and the outcast,
    who welcomed the strangers and the unloved,
    help me to welcome others in your name.
When I am touched with your love,
    give me the courage to share my story with those around me,
    and to tell my friends and neighbours
    how you have transformed the world.
Amen.

WEEK 4, TUESDAY

Is This the One?

Bible Reading

Now there was a man in Jerusalem whose name was Simeon; this man was righteous and devout, looking forward to the consolation of Israel, and the Holy Spirit rested on him. It had been revealed to him by the Holy Spirit that he would not see death before he had seen the Lord's Messiah. Guided by the Spirit, Simeon came into the temple; and when the parents brought in the child Jesus, to do for him what was customary under the law, Simeon took him in his arms and praised God, saying, "Master, now you are dismissing your servant in peace, according to your word; for my eyes have seen your salvation, which you have prepared in the presence of all peoples, a light for revelation to the Gentiles and for glory to your people Israel." And the child's father and mother were amazed at what was being said about him. Then Simeon blessed them and said to his mother Mary, "This child is destined for the falling and the rising of many in Israel, and to be a sign that will be opposed so that the inner thoughts of many will be revealed – and a sword will pierce your own soul too."

Luke 2:25-35

The Voice of Simeon

Every day I painfully dragged myself to the Temple, wondering if this would be *the day,* wondering if the child in front of me was the one who was promised in scripture, the one who would bring salvation to his people.

My name is Simeon, and like many before me and many that will come after me, I am a servant of the God of Israel. I have been all my life and will be until the day I die, which I hope will be soon. I am old, my body is wracked with pain; even breathing is becoming a struggle these days. Yet God, in his goodness, made me a promise years ago that I would not die until I had seen with my own eyes his holy one, the Lord's anointed, the Messiah.

So, day after day I went to inspect the parents and their children as they brought them to the Temple for God's blessing, and I waited for a sign that this was the one I waited for. I wasn't sure what kind of sign I was seeking – a lightning bolt, a choir of angels – but I guessed that somewhere in the very pit of my stomach I would know.

Then one day it happened. A young mother arrived with her older husband, cradling her baby boy. I knew instinctively without a shadow of doubt that this was the one who had been spoken of for generations, the one whom God himself had chosen.

I took the child in my arms and felt a deep sense of awe; I was holding the realisation of God's promise. I smiled at his parents but spoke to God: "Now, let your servant go in peace, for my eyes have seen your salvation."

To the child's mother I offered some advice and hard truths. Sadly, there was not much comfort to be found in my words. "Your son will see the rise and fall of many in Jerusalem. He will bring hope to his people and joy to those who are willing to receive him. However, your heart will be broken, as his body will be broken. Your dancing will turn to mourning for the good of all humanity."

At my words, her bright eyes clouded over. She began to cry, as the enormity of the task which lay before her began to sink in. She would be raising the only son of God.

I blessed the boy, although it was he who should have been blessing me. I blessed his earthly parents, encouraging them in all that was to come. Then I handed him back, knowing in that moment that it would not be long before I would meet God face to face. Heaven was calling me home, as my work on earth had now been completed.

Pause for Thought

- Simeon lived with the difficulties that come with old age but he still trusted God. When you experience difficulties, do you trust in him? Can you believe that he is still using you and working in your life?
- Simeon believed that God had made a promise to him. Does God make promises to us today? If so, what has he promised you?
- Simeon blessed the child Jesus. Whom could you bless today?

Action

Find a Celtic blessing.[2] Allow God to bless you through it and then share it with others so that it might bless them.

Prayer

God of promise,
    help us to believe that you work in and through all things.
Remind us in times when we are experiencing pain –
    mentally, physically or spiritually –
    that you are with us, holding us up and helping us through.
Help us to share our daily blessings with those around us,
    so that all might be blessed by you.
Amen.

---

[2] You can find some online at *www.faithandworship.com/Celtic_Blessings_and_Prayers.htm*

WEEK 4, WEDNESDAY

Joy in My Sorrow

Bible Reading

There was also a prophet, Anna the daughter of Phanuel, of the tribe of Asher. She was of a great age, having lived with her husband seven years after her marriage, then as a widow to the age of eighty-four. She never left the temple but worshiped there with fasting and prayer night and day. At that moment she came, and began to praise God and to speak about the child to all who were looking for the redemption of Jerusalem. When they had finished everything required by the law of the Lord, they returned to Galilee, to their own town of Nazareth. The child grew and became strong, filled with wisdom; and the favour of God was upon him.

Luke 2:36-40

The Voice of Anna

Despite all my sorrow, through this child I have now known joy. I have waited patiently, and I have spoken to all who would listen about the conviction of my heart and the reality of the coming Saviour. Today he has come, and I have seen with my own eyes God's salvation.

My name is Anna and I am a prophetess from the tribe of Asher. The name my parents gave me means 'favour' or 'grace', and God had granted me both in a long and varied life.

I married young and spent seven happy years with my husband, but then he died leaving me a widow, and I have remained so all my life. My sorrow was deep, and the pain of loss was etched on my face, ageing me before my years. The hope for children and a life lived in them had been cruelly snatched from me. Yet through it all, I knew that God was good, that he had chosen me and set me apart. I was just waiting for my sorrow to be turned into joy.

After my husband's death, I dedicated myself wholly to the Lord. Never leaving the Temple in Jerusalem, I spent my time worshipping, fasting and praying, offering my life back to God's service. I was offered living accommodation in the Temple due to my status as a prophetess, for which I was very grateful as, without a husband, how else would I have survived?

I worked hard and kept my head down. It was a difficult environment in which to be a woman – expected to keep silent and not to have an opinion about anything. This somewhat conflicted with my calling, to stand up and speak out about the coming Messiah.

My prayer life was the heartbeat of the Temple. When the priests led the worship, I prayed, bearing the soul of every believer to the throne-room of God. When parents brought their children for dedication, I prayed for health and hope and encouragement.

Then one day, when a certain woman brought her son to the Temple, I knew instantly that this was the one we had waited for; this was the child in whom our liberation rested, and I had been allowed to see him face to face.

I prayed for his mother who, like me, would taste bitter sorrow before the new world came. I prayed for courage, that she could brave the days ahead, as I have done – trusting in the goodness of God, believing in his unfailing promise which her son would deliver.

Over the decades, grief had become my friend. Now, through this infant, I met with joy once again and my heart was full to breaking with the love that he radiated. I am old and my body is decaying but because I have seen him, I can depart in peace; my joy is complete and sadness is banished forever.

Pause for Thought

- Have you known the pain of grief in your life?
- Were you able to find comfort in God?
- What does your prayer life look like? Can you gain encouragement from the example of Anna?

Action

Spend a little longer in prayer today than usual. Take a piece of string with you, if you have some, and tie knots in the string as you pray, to symbolise your prayers. Or, if you do not know what to say to God, just listen and allow him to speak to your heart.

Prayer

God, who accompanies us through of the joys and sorrows of life,
    draw alongside those I know who are grieving today.
    Help them to find comfort in those around them and in you.
Help me to come alongside those in pain
    and offer a helping hand when it is needed.
Teach me to pray as Anna prayed
    so that I might know your heart
    and share it with others.
Amen.

Week 4, Thursday

Star-gazing

Bible Reading

In the time of King Herod, after Jesus was born in Bethlehem of Judea, wise men from the East came to Jerusalem, asking, "Where is the child who has been born king of the Jews? For we observed his star at its rising, and have come to pay him homage." When King Herod heard this, he was frightened, and all Jerusalem with him; and calling together all the chief priests and scribes of the people, he inquired of them where the Messiah was to be born. They told him, "In Bethlehem of Judea; for so it has been written by the prophet: 'And you, Bethlehem, in the land of Judah, are by no means least among the rulers of Judah; for from you shall come a ruler who is to shepherd my people Israel.'"

Matthew 2:1-6

The Voice of a Wise Man

I guess some would say that it was all a bit foolish, with still nothing to show for it. Yet for me, it was all worth it – every mile travelled, every barrier crossed and every star followed. It changed everything. *He* changed everything. Nothing could ever be the same again. That little bundle cradled in his mother's arms – no words spoken, but in his silence, he held the world.

I was young, enthusiastic about life and willing to try anything once. I took up star-gazing; it seemed like a good idea at the time. It was all the craze back then, and I didn't want to be left out of the action.

It was one night in mid-July; we were gathered, waiting, watching the stars as always. I didn't really know one from the other, but the social life was good and I was rather attracted to the girl with the red hair.

However, on that night the girl paled into insignificance as the sky was lit by an amazing new star.

In time we came to believe that this star was a sign, and a few of us could stand it no longer. We hired some camels and set out. We had no real idea of where we would end up, nor of what we would find when we got there, but we began.

The journey was long and varied. Many times along the way we felt like giving up and just going home. Yet something drew us on! As we travelled, we continued to discover that stars we studied were telling us a story: the story of God, who created and sustained, and now, in our time, would enter our world.

We wanted to take some gifts, so we consulted the stars. We settled on gold for kingship, frankincense for burial and myrrh for anointing. If we had known we would find a child, we would have taken something else.

Eventually, after a few hiccups, like visiting the wrong king and getting lost a few times, we arrived. The star we followed stopped, not over palace or hall of fame, but over a smelly stable. There was no fanfare or army, just a young woman holding her firstborn son.

However, we were welcomed. We were strangers from a distant land, but we were not ignored or ill-treated. We were accepted and, surprisingly, so were our gifts. I guess they were worth some money, if nothing else. We had come face-to-face with the promised king, the creator of the universe, and he had welcomed us.

Pause for Thought

- The wise men went searching for Jesus. What are you searching for in life? How does Jesus fit into your hopes and dreams?
- What gifts could you offer Jesus? How can you give them to him?
- The wise men travelled a long way to offer their gifts. What will the cost be for you to offer your gifts to Jesus?

Action

The next time there is a clear sky, go outside and look at the stars. Try to imagine what it must have been like to witness the brightest star of all. Ask God in your heart whether there is a 'journey' he wants to take you on, as part of his plan for your life.

Prayer

God, who guided the wise men to Jesus by a bright star in the sky,
guide me also, that I might follow you.
Help me to give you the gift of myself this Christmas
so that you can use my life for your glory.
Amen.

Week 4, Friday

I am the King

Bible Reading

Then Herod secretly called for the wise men and learned from them the exact time when the star had appeared. Then he sent them to Bethlehem, saying, "Go and search diligently for the child; and when you have found him, bring me word so that I may also go and pay him homage." When they had heard the king, they set out; and there, ahead of them, went the star that they had seen at its rising, until it stopped over the place where the child was. When they saw that the star had stopped, they were overwhelmed with joy. On entering the house, they saw the child with Mary his mother; and they knelt down and paid him homage. Then, opening their treasure chests, they offered him gifts of gold, frankincense, and myrrh. And having been warned in a dream not to return to Herod, they left for their own country by another road.

Matthew 2:7-12

The Voice of King Herod

I am the king of the Jews. Me. No-one else has, or can have, that position. I have been appointed to rule over the kingdom of Judea by the Roman Emperor himself. No-one is about to take my title or my rule away. Just let them try…

I guess my name will go down in history for all the wrong reasons, but I haven't been all bad. I brought peace to my kingdom and ruled well, but I confess that power corrupted me and matters got rather out of hand.

I loved my wife deeply, but my advisers informed me she was plotting against me. Somewhat paranoid, I believed and trusted them over her, so

I had her killed. My sons grew big and strong, and although I was full of pride for them, I feared a takeover bid, so I had them killed too.

Then came the strangers from the East – dressed in fine clothes, with camels laden with gold and jewels. Surely, they had heard of my kingship and had come to pay homage to me? But it turned out they had not come for me at all.

"We have come to worship the newborn King of the Jews," they said. "We have seen his star in the East and we have followed it here, to praise him."

I could feel my blood boiling inside of me. Who was this imposter who dared to claim my throne? I needed to know, so I questioned them some more, then I ordered servants to make them welcome while I sought the wisdom of my priests.

"Look in your books," I commanded them. "This seems to be a religious matter, so search the scriptures and see what they tell of the Jewish Saviour. Where is he predicted to be born?"

They did as I ordered, and there it was in black and white. He was to be born in Bethlehem – the anointed one of God, who would rule with love and not an iron fist; whose weakness would be his strength; who would turn his back to the oppressor's whip and die an early death. (That last bit gave me some hope and an idea...)

I returned to the wise men and told them to go and find the child, but also to come back and tell me where I could find him so that "I too can worship him".

They left, but after a long time had passed, they had still not returned. This fuelled my anger still further; the pressure inside me built up to fever pitch. I had to do something. So in a moment of madness, I sent out a decree that all the children in Bethlehem aged two years and under should be killed.

I felt justified at the time. My position had been threatened and my crown was at risk. You would have done the same, wouldn't you?

Pause for Thought

- Have you ever been in a situation where you have experienced that 'power can corrupt'?
- Herod felt betrayed and plotted against by those closest to him. Have you experienced betrayal? How did you react?

- Herod put power before his faith in God. Is there anything in your life that hinders your faith?

Action

On a piece of paper, draw a timeline of your life – or alternatively, use a piece of string. Label the most significant events in your life, and then think what decisions you have made that had an impact (positive or negative) on those events. Consider whether your decisions have been made out of faith or out of fear. Then think about whether you have any decisions ahead of you that you might need God's help with.

Prayer

God of our history, our past, present and future,
    help me to recognise you at work in every aspect of my life.
When I am tempted to allow power or fear to affect me,
    help me to stay focused on you and your plan for me.
Help me to use my history, be it positive or negative,
    to help and positively influence others.
Amen.

Week 4, Saturday

Innocent Blood

Bible Reading

When Herod had searched for him and could not find him, he examined the guards and ordered them to be put to death. Then he went down from Judea to Caesarea and stayed there. Now Herod was angry with the people of Tyre and Sidon. So they came to him in a body; and after winning over Blastus, the king's chamberlain, they asked for a reconciliation, because their country depended on the king's country for food. On an appointed day Herod put on his royal robes, took his seat on the platform, and delivered a public address to them. The people kept shouting, "The voice of a god, and not of a mortal!" And immediately, because he had not given the glory to God, an angel of the Lord struck him down, and he was eaten by worms and died. But the word of God continued to advance and gain adherents.

Acts 12:19-24

The Voice of Ghila – the Mother of an Innocent

Word has come: the king is dead.

I guess I am supposed to feel sad, or relieved, or something, *anything.* Yet there is nothing. I only feel numb. Time has not healed; God has not softened my heart. I am still angry – as bitter and as twisted as I was on the day it happened. The king's death has just brought it all flooding back.

My name is Ghila, a name that means joy and contentment, but after that day, I have never felt joy again; I am sure I never will. I was there, you see. I am a mother of an innocent. My son was taken from me, snatched from my breast and slaughtered before my eyes; all to protect the king's position, his power, his place as king – a king whom we did not choose, a king drafted in to be a puppet for the Empire.

King Herod had listened to the words of a band of foreigners, who told of a child who would claim his rightful throne, a child who would grow and be loved, wanted and proclaimed as King and Lord, not only by the Jewish nation but by all who knew him. Fear had struck Herod's heart. So, in turn, he struck fear into ours. He sent his men with orders to kill – without discrimination. Every boy under two years old died that day, mine included.

Am I meant to believe that my child's death protected *her* child? Am I expected to accept this was all part of a wider, more elaborate plan; that God had allowed my son's death so that his might live, for some higher purpose? If I am, I don't.

Don't get me wrong, I wouldn't wish this on any mother. No parent should bury their own child. It goes against the natural order of things, doesn't it?

But it wasn't her, it was us. Mary and Joseph and their son Jesus escaped. We were the ones who bore the brunt of Herod's anger. We were the ones left without mouths at our breasts, and hearts that were broken in two.

Do I now find closure, as I hear of his death? Do my gaping wounds suddenly heal? Is my shattered life instantaneously rebuilt? No. None of it.

Will I ever learn to trust again? Love again? Hope again? If I do, maybe my hope will rest on the shoulders of the child that survived. Maybe, just maybe, somehow my son's death will not have been in vain.

Pause for Thought

- Do you know of someone who has lost a child? How do you (or how could you) talk about this painful subject?
- How could you offer the hand of friendship to someone who has experienced such a loss?
- How might you be able to offer hope in this kind of situation?

Action

The next time you go for a walk, become aware of the life around you in nature. Remember before God those who have lost children, of any age, and pray for them.

Prayer

Compassionate God,
    draw close to those I know
    who have experienced the loss of a child.
Give me the wisdom and grace to stand alongside them,
    and help me to recognise that you too felt that pain
    when your own son was executed.
When I find myself in a place of loss,
    help me to learn to grieve, to trust and to hope again,
    and to find comfort in you.
Amen.

The Hope to Come

Jesus – Name Above All Names

Jesus,
Promised Messiah,
Born in a stable
But born to be King.

Jesus,
King of kings,
Worshipped by wise men
Yet with no earthly throne.

Jesus,
Son of David,
Who came in humble triumph
To show a new way.

Jesus,
Great high priest,
Who came to fulfil the law
But not to maintain it.

Jesus,
Friend of sinners,
Who befriended the outcast
And healed the sick.

Jesus,
Wonderful counsellor,
Who washed the feet
of his disciples
To be a servant to the world.

Jesus,
Bread of life and true vine,
Who offered up himself
to feed all people
So that no one should
hunger or thirst.

Jesus,
Prince of peace,
Who, when the crowds shouted,
"Crucify!"
Prayed, "Father forgive."

Jesus,
Lamb of God,
Branded as a scapegoat
and a sacrifice offered,
A ransom paid for us all.

Jesus,
Son of man,
Who was laid
in a borrowed tomb,
Quiet and still.

Jesus,
Light of the world,
Who overcame the darkness
And ushered in a new dawn.

Jesus,
Name above all names,
Promised, ascended
and glorified,
Lead us on.

CHRISTMAS DAY

Life for Death

Bible Reading

In those days a decree went out from Emperor Augustus that all the world should be registered. This was the first registration and was taken while Quirinus was governor of Syria. All went to their own towns to be registered. Joseph also went from the town of Nazareth in Galilee to Judea, to the city of David called Bethlehem, because he was descended from the house and family of David. He went to be registered with Mary, to whom he was engaged and who was expecting a child. While they were there, the time came for her to deliver her child. And she gave birth to her firstborn son and wrapped him in bands of cloth, and laid him in a manger, because there was no place for them in the inn.

Luke 2:1-7

The Voice of Life

Jesus says:

"I am the voice of life – a life that will not die; the life that conquered death, and the life that still lives on in all who are called to bear my name. I am the life from before creation, the life that brings restoration, turning chaos and darkness into order and a light. I AM.

"I told everyone my story from beginning to end – from birth to death to rebirth. I told them what would happen, and how; that I would be arrested, tried, lashed and crucified, then buried in a borrowed tomb. Then on the third day, I would rise again, defeating sin and death.

"All this was planned. Before I was born, the scheme was set in place and foretold, even while God's people chose to walk their own path.

"I was there when God spoke. I witnessed how he breathed life into creation, including humanity. I was there when a relationship was formed, when God chose and claimed his people as his own. Then, as they chose the darkness over light, death over life, our ultimate plan came into its own.

"'I will go,' I said, 'and leave all this behind me. I will willingly trade the majesty of heaven for the chaos of the earth.'

"A young woman was chosen to bring my human form to birth. The man to whom she was engaged would become my human father and raise me to be a physical man.

"Then the time came for me – the Life – to be born and live among my people – yet without sinning. I would feel all there was to feel. I would know happiness and sorrow, hope and suffering. I would form friendships, and know betrayal and denial, loneliness and pain. Worst of all, I would experience separation from my heavenly father.

"In the shadow of the cross I was born, and my mother laid me in the food trough of a stable, wrapping me in an old blanket, because nobody could offer a room for my parents to stay in when they needed it. My birth was announced by angels, and those who came to visit were from all corners of the earth and from all walks of life.

"Shepherds came, demonstrating that I had come to all and not just those who could afford me. Wise men travelled from the East, representing the non-Jewish contingent; showing that my reign of life, hope, joy and peace would be open to all, regardless of race, creed or colour; establishing that God is accessible to all.

"'I am the voice of life,' I told those I encountered on earth. Now I offer life in all its fullness to anyone who wishes to receive me."

Pause for Thought

- In what way do you think Jesus lived his life to the full? What would it look like for *you* to be living life to the full?
- Jesus offers life in all its fullness. What does this mean and how can we take him up on this offer?
- How could you help those around you to live life to the full?

Action

The next time you go out for a walk, stop for a moment by a large tree and think about how deep the roots go into the ground to keep it standing firm, strong and healthy.

Then take a moment to consider how deep your roots are in Jesus. How much do you feed from his word? Do you allow yourself to be nourished by him to ensure that your spiritual life is strong and healthy?

Prayer

God of life,
  help me to receive your gift that is freely given in Christ.
Help me then to take it out and show your love and life
  to all people, regardless of race, colour or creed.
Enable me to live a life for you that demonstrates to others
  the life you want to give.
Amen.

BOXING DAY

The Baptist's Cry

Bible Reading

He said, "I am the voice of one crying out in the wilderness, 'Make straight the way of the Lord,'" as the prophet Isaiah said. Now they had been sent from the Pharisees. They asked him, "Why then are you baptizing if you are neither the Messiah, nor Elijah, nor the prophet?" John answered them, "I baptize with water. Among you stands one whom you do not know, the one who is coming after me; I am not worthy to untie the thong of his sandal." This took place in Bethany across the Jordan where John was baptizing. The next day he saw Jesus coming toward him and declared, "Here is the Lamb of God who takes away the sin of the world! This is he of whom I said, 'After me comes a man who ranks ahead of me because he was before me.' I myself did not know him; but I came baptizing with water for this reason, that he might be revealed to Israel." And John testified, "I saw the Spirit descending from heaven like a dove, and it remained on him. I myself did not know him, but the one who sent me to baptize with water said to me, 'He on whom you see the Spirit descend and remain is the one who baptizes with the Holy Spirit.' And I myself have seen and have testified that this is the Son of God."

John 1:23-34

If you have time, you could read the whole of John 1.

The Voice of John the Baptist

Come and join me on the banks of the river. Come and hear the words of repentance and hope. Come and be ready to engage with radical transformation. For I have a life-changing message to proclaim from a powerful God.

My parents named me John – not because they wanted to but because that was what God told them to do. When I was old enough to understand, my mother told me how I had leapt inside her when I first encountered my cousin in the womb of his mother Mary.

The two of us played as children, boyhood games that brought laughter to our faces, but all too soon we grew into men and went our separate ways. He went to work as a carpenter in his father's firm and I was to wander in the wilderness until the appointed time.

That time is now, for I stand ready to fulfil all that was written about me by the prophets. I have been set aside to prepare a way for the Lord, to make the path straight, to level the bumps and fill in the potholes. I have been instructed to make ready the hearts of many, so that they may see and recognise the Messiah in their midst.

I look different from others around me, with unkempt hair and an untidy beard. I live a simple life, eating locusts and wild honey, and my clothing is neither refined nor fine. Some say I am wild, others say I am mad, while still others see the truth; they see past the extremes and see a man called by God to be a messenger of hope in our time.

My stage is the river Jordan and the performance will challenge your attitudes and values. The journey I will take you on is fast, and the effects will last forever. I will take you from dry to wet, from dirty to clean, from sinful to forgiven and from death to life. I offer you a dunking in water, a symbol of dying to an old life and rising to a new one with God.

However, my baptism is just the beginning; for the one who comes after me will baptise with the Holy Spirit and with fire. I am just a stagehand compared to the star of the show who will come. His light will shine brighter than a beacon and his love will warm the coldest of hearts.

So get ready, all of you who claim to be God's people, and even those who don't. When he comes, there will be no distinction; all will be welcomed and valued, and no one will be turned away.

Look, here he comes, the Lamb of God who takes away the sins of the world, Jesus of Nazareth, the Son of God…

Pause for Thought

- Have you ever been asked to prepare for an event or someone's arrival? How did you feel to see your preparations come to fruition? How do you think John must have felt to recognise Jesus?
- What can you do to help prepare people's hearts to recognise and receive Jesus?
- John looked and acted differently to those around him. How do you treat those around you who look and act differently?

Action

Get a bowl of water and a stone. Imagine the stone covered with all the bad things (sins) in your life, everything that separates you from God. Now drop the stone into the bowl. Remember how all those sins have been washed away and that God is offering you and all people a new start with him.

Prayer

God of hope and forgiveness,
help me to understand that because of Jesus
my sins can be washed away,
and I can stand forgiven before you.
Help me, like John, to speak boldly about you,
preparing the way for you in the hearts of those I meet today.
Amen.

December 27th

I Dried My Tears with My Hair

Bible Reading

One of the Pharisees asked Jesus to eat with him, and he went into the Pharisee's house and took his place at the table. And a woman in the city, who was a sinner, having learned that he was eating in the Pharisee's house, brought an alabaster jar of ointment. She stood behind him at his feet, weeping, and began to bathe his feet with her tears and to dry them with her hair. Then she continued kissing his feet and anointing them with the ointment. Now when the Pharisee who had invited him saw it, he said to himself, "If this man were a prophet, he would have known who and what kind of woman this is who is touching him – that she is a sinner."

Luke 7:36-39

The Voice of a Sinful Woman

Everyone considered me an outcast. They made sure I that I knew my place, firmly at the bottom of the pile.

As a woman, I was on a sticky wicket to begin with. On top of that, I had also been branded a sinner. I confess I had not always followed all their rules to the letter, or gone along with their agendas, but a girl's got to eat.

I had heard about this man, Jesus. People had said that he sat down with sinners, ate with tax collectors, and even befriended people like me, treating us as equals and offering us forgiveness and a new beginning. I wanted that – a chance to change, to leave my old life behind and start again.

I knew that his friends would not let me anywhere near him, so I kept my ears to the ground and waited for a chance to meet him. Then I heard about a dinner being hosted by one of the local dignitaries. I turned up, batted my eyelids at the bouncer on the door and walked in. I wanted to see Jesus and knew that I would do anything in my power to make that happen.

Suddenly, there he was, reclining at the table with the other guests. I could wait no longer; this was it. I ran, hit the floor and poured oil from my jar all over his feet.

As I did this, I began to cry uncontrollably, as the weight of my sin fell away from me. My tears mingled with the perfume, and I wiped his feet with my hair.

There was uproar, but not from him; he just smiled and cradled my face in his hands. Someone complained that the perfume was expensive and could have been sold and the money given to the poor. Jesus pointed out that, sadly, there would always be poor people, but he would not be around forever.

Someone was quick to highlight my poor reputation, but Jesus commended me for preparing him for burial. Of course, that had not been my intention, but I was pleased that he liked what I had done. I was condemned by dinner guests and hosts alike, but Jesus forgave me and gave me back my life.

I left the party, escorted out by the bullish bouncer, but it had all been worth it. I had seen Jesus. I had washed his feet with my perfume and my tears, and dried them with my hair.

So, what next? Would I go back to the way things always had been, with men, and money and dodgy dealings, or would life now change? I had been transformed, and I decided that from that moment on, my very existence would reflect Jesus' light.

Pause for Thought

- Have you ever felt like an outcast?
- Would you be transformed through meeting Jesus?
- What does forgiveness mean for you?

Action

The next time you repair something in your home, or maybe your car, let it be a reminder of how Jesus repairs lives. He does not just discard us and replace us; each one of us is precious to him and loved by him. Do you feel you need to be repaired? Tell him about it.

Prayer

God of the outcast, stranger and refugee,
    thank you that you promise to be with me
    when I suffer rejection or even persecution.
Help those who are persecuted for following Christ
    to stand firm in their faith in you.
Help me to reach out to those
    who are seen in society as outcasts.
I gratefully receive the forgiveness you offer for my sins;
    help me to show that same forgiveness to others.
Amen.

DECEMBER 28TH

Under the Cover of Darkness

Bible Reading

Now there was a Pharisee named Nicodemus, a leader of the Jews. He came to Jesus by night and said to him, "Rabbi, we know that you are a teacher who has come from God; for no one can do these signs that you do apart from the presence of God." Jesus answered him, "Very truly, I tell you, no one can see the kingdom of God without being born from above." Nicodemus said to him, "How can anyone be born after having grown old? Can one enter a second time into the mother's womb and be born?" Jesus answered, "Very truly, I tell you, no one can enter the kingdom of God without being born of water and Spirit. What is born of the flesh is flesh, and what is born of the Spirit is spirit. Do not be astonished that I said to you, 'You must be born from above.' The wind blows where it chooses, and you hear the sound of it, but you do not know where it comes from or where it goes. So it is with everyone who is born of the Spirit." Nicodemus said to him, "How can these things be?" Jesus answered him, "Are you a teacher of Israel, and yet you do not understand these things?

John 3:1-10

If you have time, you could read onwards to verse 20.

The Voice of Nicodemus

I was there when they took his lifeless body down from the cross, beaten and blooded. It seemed like all hope had gone then; not like before, when I had skulked off to see him man-to-man under the cover of darkness.

My name is Nicodemus, and I am a Pharisees and a ruler of the Jews. I taught in the Temple and in some small way tried to bridge the gap between God and his people. However, some time ago now, a new man appeared on the scene – a man who claimed that he himself was the bridge and that only through him could God be reached.

I listened from the sidelines to his stories and his claims, witnessed first-hand the miracles he performed. I also heard the anger mounting against him from my friends and colleagues in the Temple. He was putting noses out of joint, and those in positions of leadership were feeling threatened.

Nevertheless, he spoke with authority, and I for one wanted to know more. I told him that I knew he was a teacher sent from God. How else could he perform such amazing acts of healing and deliverance? I dared to ask him if there was more to his claim than merely words.

He told me that I had to be born again. *Crazy!* How can someone re-enter their mother's womb and be born a second time? He smiled at my question and took time to explain it to me. He did not mean physical birth, as that would be impossible; he meant being born of God's Holy Spirit – a spiritual birth.

I know my scriptures. I have read about how the Spirit of God hovered over the waters at the creation of the world, how the Spirit of wisdom inspired and filled the prophets of old. Now this man, this Jesus, was offering me that same Spirit.

He spoke of the "serpent in the desert" – a story I know well, in which Moses saved God's people from being bitten by snakes. At Moses' word, a bronze snake had been lifted skyward on a pole, securing their freedom. It was only later, as Jesus was lifted on a cross, that I understood. Jesus claimed that through his death he would save people, just like Moses saved people in his time.

Now that I have seen him die, I am convinced that every word of his claim is true. I no longer hide under the cover of darkness; I want to follow him. I want to be counted as his. I used my wealth to buy and bring spices to bind the body and bury him according to our customs.

I have been touched by God's Holy Spirit. Therefore, I can no longer stay the same. I cannot remain silent. I will nail my colours to the mast and claim my reward in heaven.

Pause for Thought

- Why do you think Nicodemus went to Jesus under the cover of darkness?
- Do you believe you have been touched by God's Holy Spirit?
- How can you respond to that?

Action

The following exercise can be done alone but could be a fun activity with family or friends.

Gather together some materials of your choice (e.g. paper and cartons to be recycled) and use them to try to build a bridge. If you want, you could try to make the bridge strong enough to carry a reasonably heavy object.

Now think about how Jesus Christ is the ultimate bridge between God and his people. Think also about how you might be a bridge for others to find their way to God.

Prayer

God, you offered us a bridge to yourself through Christ;
help me similarly to be a bridge for others
so that they too might experience the joy of knowing you.
Fill me again with your Holy Spirit
so that I will be inspired and ready to speak for you
in all the ups and downs of life.
Amen.

DECEMBER 29TH

Another Roll of the Dice

Bible Reading

At that moment the curtain of the temple was torn in two, from top to bottom. The earth shook, and the rocks were split. The tombs also were opened, and many bodies of the saints who had fallen asleep were raised. After his resurrection they came out of the tombs and entered the holy city and appeared to many. Now when the centurion and those with him, who were keeping watch over Jesus, saw the earthquake and what took place, they were terrified and said, "Truly this man was God's Son!" Many women were also there, looking on from a distance; they had followed Jesus from Galilee and had provided for him. Among them were Mary Magdalene, and Mary the mother of James and Joseph, and the mother of the sons of Zebedee.

Matthew 27:51-56

The Voice of Marco – a Roman Soldier

It was just another roll of dice, or so I thought. Just another game. Another criminal crucified. Another day at the office. But I was wrong.

I was on execution duty that day – not my favourite part of the job, but we all had to take our turn. The prisoners had been placed into our hands at the city gate, and it was our responsibility to escort them to the Place of the Skull and crucify them there. There were three of them that day, two others and *him*.

Who was he, this man from Galilee, who had succeeded in bringing the wrath of the whole Jewish nation upon himself and the rage of Rome? Who was he, this man who, when the crowd shouted, "Crucify!", asked

God to forgive them? Who was he, this man who, when we drove nails into his hands and feet, said we did not know what we were doing?

We lifted him skyward, pinned to a wooden cross. It was our role. We were obeying orders. How could we do anything else? We had bills to pay, families to feed and quotas to meet. It was just another roll of the dice, but the question of his identity hung heavy on my mind.

The crowd shouted. The priests mocked. Several women wept, and we played dice, gambling for his coat.

He cried out that he was thirsty. I took a sponge, soaked it in vinegar, put it on a stick and lifted it to his mouth. His broken eyes met mine. I was transfixed; it was almost as if through his agony, he smiled at me.

Suddenly, it was not just another roll of the dice, another game; it was real. Something new had begun inside me; I was being changed.

As he bowed his head and died, somehow I found life – fresh hope sparking within me, forgiveness offered freely, grace given abundantly.

Who was this man who changed our game into reality, who rolled a different die and, through his death, gave me life?

Every Jewish prophecy had been fulfilled, every dream had been realised and everyone, including me, finally had a chance to see his identity revealed.

Truly this man was the Son of God.

Pause for Thought

- Have you ever thought of life as a game?
- What gambles have you taken in life, and have they paid off?
- Marco perceived Jesus to be the Son of God. Who do you believe Jesus was/is?

Action

The next time you play a game which involves rolling dice, think about the experiences of the Roman soldiers who gambled for what little Jesus had.

Prayer

God of the Romans and the Jews, God of all people,
    today I remember the sacrifice made for us by your son;
    his life laid down so that I could be forgiven for all wrongdoing.
Help me to forgive others
    and show me how to love even those I find it hard to love.
Teach me your compassion
    and help me to learn and grow in you.
Amen.

DECEMBER 30TH

How Our Hearts Burned Within Us

Bible Reading

Now on that same day two of them were going to a village called Emmaus, about seven miles from Jerusalem, and talking with each other about all these things that had happened. While they were talking and discussing, Jesus himself came near and went with them, but their eyes were kept from recognizing him. … When he was at the table with them, he took bread, blessed and broke it, and gave it to them. Then their eyes were opened, and they recognized him; and he vanished from their sight. They said to each other, "Were not our hearts burning within us while he was talking to us on the road, while he was opening the scriptures to us?"

Luke 24:13-16,30-32

If you have time, you could read the whole of chapter 24.

The Voice of Sarah, Cleopas' Wife.

How our hearts burned within us as we turned and ran back towards Jerusalem. We had experienced a great miracle and were desperate to share it with others. However, I am getting ahead of myself; let me start at the beginning.

It had been a week full of intense emotions. Our friend and master, dare I say *Lord,* had been taken from us. At the outset, he had ridden triumphantly into the city of Jerusalem. The people had loved him; they even hailed him as their king – although hearts, minds and loyalties were soon swayed. A few words from a priest or two, a threatening look from Roman soldier and the same crowd shouted, "Crucify!" Jesus was arrested, tried, put to death and buried even before the Sabbath began.

So, there was nothing left for us in Jerusalem, and while it was still dark we headed home. We had hit rock bottom; we didn't know where to turn, and even his stories that had seemed so vivid began to fade in our memories.

At first we walked by ourselves in silence, but later we were joined by a man. He noticed our tear-stained faces and questioned us. He appeared to have no idea about the events that had unfolded. I don't know how he could have missed them!

He listened intently to our tale. Then he explained the scriptures to us, pointing out how they connected with our story. He was amazing, so full of knowledge, inspiring us to breathe again.

Eventually, we reached our destination. He indicated that he would go on, but with night fast approaching we urged him to stay. So he agreed, and we shared a meal at which he blessed and broke the bread we ate.

At that moment, to our astonishment, his identity become clear. Here was Jesus, our Lord and master – alive and present with us, just as he had promised he would be. He immediately disappeared, leaving us to reassess all that had been, all that now was and all that was to come. We had just encountered the risen Christ and that demanded a response.

We could hardly believe it, but still half-dazed we headed back to the city. Our hopes had been renewed. Our spirits soared and our hearts burned within us like fires. We were full of joy, ready and eager to testify that Jesus Christ was alive, even willing at that moment to die if we had to – determined to share the good news.

Pause for Thought

- Have you ever had the experience of your heart 'burning' within you? What led to that moment and what followed?
- Why do you think that Jesus was recognised when he broke the bread?
- The friends felt compelled to go and share their news. How could you share the good news about Jesus?

Action

Is there a Bible verse or passage you could share with a family member or friends that would encourage them in their current situation? Go ahead and share it! Then imagine how it might have felt to be on that road to Emmaus when Jesus opened the scriptures to his friends.

Prayer

God who walked alongside his friends on the road to Emmaus,
opening the scriptures to them,
open them for me as well,
so that I might be as fired up and inspired as they were.
Give me a passion to share your story with everyone I meet,
and a heart to bring others to you.
Amen.

NEW YEAR'S EVE

Breakfast on the Beach

Bible Reading

After these things Jesus showed himself again to the disciples by the Sea of Tiberias; and he showed himself in this way. Gathered there together were Simon Peter, Thomas called the Twin, Nathanael of Cana in Galilee, the sons of Zebedee, and two others of his disciples. Simon Peter said to them, "I am going fishing." They said to him, "We will go with you." They went out and got into the boat, but that night they caught nothing. Just after daybreak, Jesus stood on the beach; but the disciples did not know that it was Jesus. Jesus said to them, "Children, you have no fish, have you?" They answered him, "No." He said to them, "Cast the net to the right side of the boat, and you will find some." So they cast it, and now they were not able to haul it in because there were so many fish. That disciple whom Jesus loved said to Peter, "It is the Lord!" When Simon Peter heard that it was the Lord, he put on some clothes, for he was naked, and jumped into the sea. But the other disciples came in the boat, dragging the net full of fish, for they were not far from the land, only about a hundred yards off. When they had gone ashore, they saw a charcoal fire there, with fish on it, and bread. Jesus said to them, "Bring some of the fish that you have just caught." So Simon Peter went aboard and hauled the net ashore, full of large fish, a hundred fifty-three of them; and though there were so many, the net was not torn. Jesus said to them, "Come and have breakfast." Now none of the disciples dared to ask him, "Who are you?" because they knew it was the Lord.

John 21:1-12

Try reading the whole of John 21 if you have the opportunity.

The Voice of Peter

Hope – let me tell you about hope. Hope was born, hope died and hope was reborn in the person of Jesus. Now hope lives on in me, as I try to mirror the life he lived.

My name is Peter and I was a fisherman. I guess you could say I still am, but now I fish for people instead. Let me tell you my story.

About three years ago, a stranger approached me on the shore and asked me if he could use my boat. I agreed, thinking he was going fishing, but no. Instead, he stood up and preached to the gathered crowd, inviting them to embark on a personal relationship with God. The man was called Jesus.

"Come," he said to me, "leave your nets, leave your family and friends, and follow me."

There was something about him, something compelling, and I was drawn in. I followed, and as I did I began a journey from which there was no return, where hope began to live and breathe again.

Jesus' other followers and I travelled around the country, increasing in number and gathering momentum. We watched as Jesus healed the sick, cleansed the lepers and gave sight to the blind. We listened as he painted pictures with his words of a new kingdom built on equality and love, which he would usher in.

As time went on, you could cut the tension with a knife, as conspiring whispers grew louder. He was making the chief priests nervous. He was challenging their positions and shaking their temples of power.

At Passover, we entered the city to a hero's welcome. We shared a meal together, as we had done many times before. But this time he likened the bread to his body and the wine to his blood poured out.

Under the cover of darkness, soldiers drew near. They bound him and led him away to face a cruel and corrupt form of justice. Then they beat him, placed a heavy beam on his shoulders and led him to a hill outside the city, where they executed him.

After his death, in desperation, I went back to what I knew – taking solace in my nets but catching nothing. Then, seemingly out of nowhere, there appeared a barbecue lit on the beach – fish cooking on an open fire, and Jesus' tender voice: "Peter, will you feed my sheep? Peter, be the rock on which I build my church."

I had breakfast on the beach with my Lord. I had not always been faithful to him, particularly when he had been arrested, but I was now forgiven, restored, reinstated, commissioned and sent out. Now hope lives on and will never die.

Pause for Thought

- Peter was unfaithful to Jesus. Have there been times when you have hidden being a Christian?
- Peter found himself forgiven and reinstated. God offers you (and me) the same today? How do you feel about that?
- Peter enjoyed breakfast on the beach with his Lord. Jesus wants us the experience the same intimate relationship. How can you respond to that today?

Action

Consider inviting some friends around to enjoy a meal together. As you enjoy each other's company and eating with one another, be reminded that this kind of intimate relationship is offered to you by God, if you invite him into your heart.

Prayer

Dear Lord, you call me to join you for breakfast on the beach!
    Help me to become aware of the closeness of your love for me.
Help me to draw close to those around me and offer them
    the kind of friendship you want to have with all people.
Help me to live and grow in you
    so that I too can be your hands and feet
    where I live and work in this season of life.
Amen.

NEW YEAR'S DAY

They Hurled Stones at Him

Bible Reading

When they heard these things, they became enraged and ground their teeth at Stephen. But filled with the Holy Spirit, he gazed into heaven and saw the glory of God and Jesus standing at the right hand of God. "Look," he said, "I see the heavens opened and the Son of Man standing at the right hand of God!" But they covered their ears, and with a loud shout all rushed together against him. Then they dragged him out of the city and began to stone him; and the witnesses laid their coats at the feet of a young man named Saul. While they were stoning Stephen, he prayed, "Lord Jesus, receive my spirit." Then he knelt down and cried out in a loud voice, "Lord, do not hold this sin against them." When he had said this, he died.

Acts 7:54-60

It is well worth reading the preceding events in Acts 6 if you have time.

The Voice of Timon, Friend of Stephen

After Jesus' death and resurrection, the early church grew. The Holy Spirit was convicting people of their sins, and they were turning back to God. In fact, there were so many conversions that the apostles couldn't keep up with demand. They prayed and asked God to identify five others who could help to take some of the load. Stephen and I were two of those chosen. We had hands laid upon us, and we were set apart to lead and teach God's people.

Our numbers in the church continued to increase. People from all walks of life were becoming disciples of Jesus Christ. With God's power, Stephen and I were performing wonders and signs among the people.

However, there were those that launched attacks against us, and some looked for any reason to have us arrested and put to death. They stirred up the crowd and it was not long before Stephen stood bound before them. Like his Lord before him, he faced a trumped-up charge.

Stephen was outstanding. He retold God's story for them, beginning with Abraham, through Isaac and Jacob, to their freedom from slavery by Moses. He didn't stop there either! He told of the handing down of the Ten Commandments, the people's disobedience and the need for a Saviour who would redeem his people.

Instead of understanding, Stephen was met with fury, and his accusers roared in rage. Yet he did not fear; he was convinced that Jesus stood at the right hand of God in heaven and that he would know his protection.

The people covered their ears. They did not want to listen. They had made their decision: *Stephen had to die.* They rushed him, dragged him out of the city and began to stone him. I watched as stone after stone hit his body, driving him to the ground and piercing his flesh. But as all this happened, I heard him praying that God would receive his spirit and forgive those that had hurled their weapons of torture. Finally, he breathed his last, the crowd left, and I tended to his lifeless, blooded corpse.

Stephen had sung God's praises right until the last. He had not wavered from his faith or his conviction. He had stood and been counted for Christ. I just hope that if I ever find myself chained and facing death, that I too will stay faithful and go down fighting for what I believe in...

The crowd had hurled their stones at Stephen and his only crime had been to preach Christ crucified. Through the death of my friend, I saw what true faith looked like, and I pray for strength and courage so that I may live a life like his.

Pause for Thought

- Why do you think so many came to believe in Christ in those early years?
- Stephen retold God's story to the people. How often do you tell your story of faith? Could you pray for more opportunities to do so?
- In the face of death, Stephen's faith did not falter. What do you think gave him such courage? Would you be able to do the same?

Action

Find a stone, pick it up and take a good look at it. Try to imagine what it might have been like to be stoned to death. Think about Stephen and what he went through for the sake of sharing his belief in Jesus. Maybe you could ask God to increase your courage and boldness in sharing the story of Jesus with others.

Prayer

God of the oppressed,
  I pray for those who are suffering torture around the world;
  cause their oppressors to become aware
  that their behaviour is unacceptable.
Be with those across the world who are not allowed
  to share their faith openly.
Today I thank you for the freedom of belief and speech
  that we are granted in this country.
Amen.

JANUARY 2ND

Never Too Near or Far

Bible Reading

Now those who were scattered went from place to place, proclaiming the word. Philip went down to the city of Samaria and proclaimed the Messiah to them. The crowds with one accord listened eagerly to what was said by Philip, hearing and seeing the signs that he did, for unclean spirits, crying with loud shrieks, came out of many who were possessed; and many others who were paralyzed or lame were cured. So there was great joy in that city. ... Then an angel of the Lord said to Philip, "Get up and go toward the south to the road that goes down from Jerusalem to Gaza." (This is a wilderness road.) So he got up and went. Now there was an Ethiopian eunuch, a court official of the Candace, queen of the Ethiopians, in charge of her entire treasury. He had come to Jerusalem to worship and was returning home; seated in his chariot, he was reading the prophet Isaiah. Then the Spirit said to Philip, "Go over to this chariot and join it." So Philip ran up to it and heard him reading the prophet Isaiah. He asked, "Do you understand what you are reading?" He replied, "How can I, unless someone guides me?" And he invited Philip to get in and sit beside him. ... As they were going along the road, they came to some water; and the eunuch said, "Look, here is water! What is to prevent me from being baptized?" He commanded the chariot to stop, and both of them, Philip and the eunuch, went down into the water, and Philip baptized him. When they came up out of the water, the Spirit of the Lord snatched Philip away; the eunuch saw him no more, and went on his way rejoicing.

Acts 8:4-8,26-31,36-39

For the complete story, read the whole of Acts 8.

The Voice of Philip the Evangelist

It all began when I was a young man. Jesus was preaching in my town and I liked what I heard. Here was a man unlike any other. He spoke with authority and invited us into a personal relationship with God. None of our other teachers did that. I tagged along – not part of his inner circle, but still one of the seventy-two he sent out to spread his message.

I watched the drama of that fateful weekend from the sidelines, not really sure what to make of it all. I was sad and disappointed. Like everyone else, I had hoped he was the one, you see. Yet, death was not the end for him, nor for us. In fact, it was just the beginning. When resurrection came, hope was rekindled and the early church began to grow.

The church grew so fast that Jesus' chosen few could no longer cope, so they drafted in others and I was one of them. I was faithful and did my best to serve God and his people. Then one day, out of the blue, I felt I heard God speak to me. There was no blinding light or rush of wind, just a gentle whisper deep inside my soul: "Leave this place," the voice said. "Go to the wilderness road and I will meet you there."

I went without question. There, as promised, God met me. As I waited, a man from Ethiopia rode up in a carriage. He was reading from the Bible, from the book of Isaiah, but from his face I could see he had no clue what it was about. I smiled at him, and something in my eyes invited him to ask his questions.

He wanted to know of whom the prophet Isaiah spoke: himself or another? Then question after question came my way.

I just listened. I felt God telling me, "Hold off, let him speak. It will be your turn soon."

Eventually the man did stop.

"Would you like me to explain this to you?" I asked.

His smile said it all, no need for words. So I told him all about Jesus: how he had been sent by God to live among his people; how he had preached and taught and healed; how he had been arrested and killed, and how he had risen, conquering death. I told him of God's Holy Spirit that had formerly descended on just a few but now was offered to all. I explained how believers could be baptised and washed clean. Then I stopped, allowing him time to take it all in.

Again he smiled. “Stop the coach!” he instructed. Then, turning to me, he said, “Here is water – what is stopping me being baptised right here and now?”

And that’s just what we did – right there and then; in a muddy puddle at the side of the wilderness road, the Ethiopian gave his life to Jesus. Through God’s prompting, I was in the right place at the right time. God is never too far away.

Pause for Thought

- Have you ever felt prompted to go somewhere, or call someone, and it turned out to be just right?
- God is never too far away from us. How do you feel about that?
- God sent Philip to the wilderness road. Where in the world might God be sending you?

Action

Look at a map of the world – if you don’t have an atlas, you could use Google Maps. Pray for those people whom God has sent out as missionaries to various places. Are there places you would be willing to go if God asked you? Are there places you would be *unwilling* to go if God asked you? Consider for a moment why you think that.

Prayer

God of Philip and the Ethiopian,
    help me to remember that you are never far away.
Help me to listen to your prompting and to act on it accordingly.
I pray for all those who have been called as missionaries
    to different parts of the world;
    protect them and provide for them,
    and help me to be ready to go wherever you might lead.
Amen.

January 3rd

An Ambassador in Chains

Bible Reading

Meanwhile Saul, still breathing threats and murder against the disciples of the Lord, went to the high priest and asked him for letters to the synagogues at Damascus, so that if he found any who belonged to the Way, men or women, he might bring them bound to Jerusalem. Now as he was going along and approaching Damascus, suddenly a light from heaven flashed around him. He fell to the ground and heard a voice saying to him, "Saul, Saul, why do you persecute me?" He asked, "Who are you, Lord?" The reply came, "I am Jesus, whom you are persecuting. But get up and enter the city, and you will be told what you are to do." The men who were traveling with him stood speechless because they heard the voice but saw no one. Saul got up from the ground, and though his eyes were open, he could see nothing; so they led him by the hand and brought him into Damascus.

Acts 9:1-8

If you have time, see how the story continues by reading the rest of Acts 9.

The Voice of Paul

Here I am, an 'ambassador in chains', and as I look through these prison bars and hear the jingle of keys, I know my time on earth is almost done. I sit and wait for death, but as I do, I gain life. As my thoughts wander, I recall my complete turnaround on account of *him,* the only Son of God.

As a boy, my faith was very important to me. I knew the scriptures back-to-front and front-to-back and lived by them as best I could. I had been told a story of a woman and the baby born in a manger, but that was just a fairy tale, wasn't it? As I grew, though, I also heard of the man whom people said had been sent from God. He spoke with authority and healed the sick. Eventually, the Romans executed him by nailing him to a cross. His teachings threatened to bring the whole Jewish nation into conflict with Rome, but his blasphemy had died with him – or so I thought. However, his followers claimed he was alive. They insisted that God had raised him from the dead, causing a transforming movement to arise.

I stood up for Israel, gathered some men around me and sought a commission to kill or incarcerate anyone that followed him. Then I set off on my way to Damascus to stamp out the uprising.

Suddenly, I was hit by a blinding light so powerful that I fell to my knees and hid my eyes. When I finally looked up, I could see nothing. I had been struck blind.

In my darkness, I heard a voice.

"Who's there and what do you want with me?" I asked.

"I am Jesus, whom you persecute," came the reply. "Now, get up, go to the city and tell my friends I have chosen you to be a light and a hope to unbelievers."

I was terrified, but I did as I was told; aided by my men, I stumbled into the city.

Eventually, a man came. He healed my eyes and listened to my story; from there everything changed. I no longer sought to kill and destroy the followers of Christ, for now I was one of them myself. Instead of persecuting others, I suffered persecution of my own, as from shipwreck to shipwreck, from prison cell to prison cell, I learnt what it meant to lean on God. I stood in chains before Romans and Jews, knowing Jesus would never leave me. For he had promised that once I believed in him, I would never walk alone.

So now, as death approaches, I wait as an 'ambassador in chains' to greet my Lord; to be received at the gates of heaven; to be embraced; to be welcomed home and to hear those words, "Well done, my good and faithful servant." I have 'run the race' that was set before me by Christ. I have given all for the sake of the gospel, and now I will go to glory in confidence and with joy.

Pause for Thought

- Why do you think Paul's views of Jesus changed so suddenly?
- Can you identify a conversion moment in your life? If so, do you talk about it?
- What does it mean for you to be part of the body of Christ?

Action

Close your eyes and imagine what it would feel like to live your life in blindness. Are there aspects of your life about which you might be blind? How could you seek help from others? And how might you help others in areas where they are blind?

Prayer

God of radical transformation,
  open the eyes of my heart so that I will see more clearly
  those around me that need a helping hand.
Help me to be an ambassador of your story,
  sharing this message of love and peace with all people.
Amen.

January 4th

What a Week it Was

Bible Reading

In Caesarea there was a man named Cornelius, a centurion of the Italian Cohort, as it was called. He was a devout man who feared God with all his household; he gave alms generously to the people and prayed constantly to God. One afternoon at about three o'clock he had a vision in which he clearly saw an angel of God coming in and saying to him, "Cornelius." He stared at him in terror and said, "What is it, Lord?" He answered, "Your prayers and your alms have ascended as a memorial before God. Now send men to Joppa for a certain Simon who is called Peter; he is lodging with Simon, a tanner, whose house is by the seaside." When the angel who spoke to him had left, he called two of his slaves and a devout soldier from the ranks of those who served him, and after telling them everything, he sent them to Joppa.

Acts 10:1-8

You could read the whole of Acts 10 if you have time.

The Voice of Cornelius

What week it was – the week when everything changed, when my prayer life become real, when I came into a relationship with God through his son Jesus.

My name is Cornelius, and I am a centurion in the Roman army. I have always been a devout man and spent much time in reflection and prayer in my younger years. I had a strong sense of duty, giving money to the poor and living in fear of God. However, my life was turned upside down by a visit from an angel and an encounter with a man of God.

I was sitting in my room praying, when all at once it was illuminated by a powerful light and there before my eyes was an angel, a messenger of God.

As you can probably imagine, I was terrified.

He reassured me – told me that my generosity towards the poor and my constant prayers had been noticed by God. He instructed me to send for a man who was staying in the city of Joppa and all would be revealed.

As soon as he left, I did as he had said and sent my men to find the man called Peter. I discovered later that God had also spoken to him, preparing the way, as normally Jews and Romans keep themselves to themselves and never mix. Within days he was on my doorstep.

Although my house was full of people I had invited to hear Peter, I ran out to meet him. There I fell at his feet and worshiped him. If God had bothered to send me an angel, surely this man was something. But he gently took me by the shoulders and told me to stand.

"I am just a man, like you," he said. "Why have you invited me to come?"

As we went inside, I told him my story and he told me his: a story about a man named Jesus, whom the Romans had crucified but God had brought back to life. I was transfixed by his tale and began to cry uncontrollably as I listened, like a baby.

I had been touched by the Holy Spirit, who convinced me of my sin and allowed me to make a fresh start. In fact, all of us who had gathered to listen to Peter were filled with God's Spirit. Peter seemed amazed to see that this Spirit was available to all people now and not just the Jewish race. "Bring water," he quickly directed. "As all these people have been filled with the Holy Spirit, what is stopping them being baptised?"

So right there, my whole household and I received the outward sign of our inner conversion. Now I pledged my life to work for – and praise – Jesus Christ, the living Son of God.

Pause for Thought

- Cornelius gave money to the poor. How might you, together with others, help the poor in your community?
- What does it mean to be baptised? Why is it important?
- Have you been baptised? If not, is this a step forward you could take in your faith?

Action

Make an effort to attend the next baptismal service. When you are there, consider how Cornelius must have felt to be baptised. God welcomed Gentiles into his family, who were considered unclean and sinners. Consider how today there is nobody outside the reach of his love.

Prayer

God of all people, rich and poor, male and female,
help me to remember that you died for all.
I choose to commit to a life lived in you so that, like Peter,
I can share the good news of your resurrection with others.
Amen.

JANUARY 5TH

The Armour of God

Bible Reading

Finally, be strong in the Lord and in the strength of his power. Put on the whole armour of God, so that you may be able to stand against the wiles of the devil. For our struggle is not against enemies of blood and flesh, but against the rulers, against the authorities, against the cosmic powers of this present darkness, against the spiritual forces of evil in the heavenly places. Therefore take up the whole armour of God, so that you may be able to withstand on that evil day, and having done everything, to stand firm. Stand therefore, and fasten the belt of truth around your waist, and put on the breastplate of righteousness. As shoes for your feet put on whatever will make you ready to proclaim the gospel of peace. With all of these, take the shield of faith, with which you will be able to quench all the flaming arrows of the evil one. Take the helmet of salvation, and the sword of the Spirit, which is the word of God. Pray in the Spirit at all times in every prayer and supplication. To that end keep alert and always persevere in supplication for all the saints. Pray also for me, so that when I speak, a message may be given to me to make known with boldness the mystery of the gospel, for which I am an ambassador in chains. Pray that I may declare it boldly, as I must speak.

Ephesians 6:10-20

The Voice of Adin – a member of the Ephesian church

So, what do you do when it feels like the whole world is falling down around you; when the storms of life are closing in; when the faith you built your existence on begins to waver? What then?

It was all so easy at the beginning: following the teachings of Jesus; learning what it meant to be a disciple where I was, a member of the Ephesian church; pleading my cause with family and friends, and even with those I met on the street; day by day growing in confidence and faith as I watched crowds come to know God.

But it wasn't long before opposition grew from both Roman and Jewish authorities. The threat of imprisonment and death increased, and the temptation to deny all I believed in deepened. It was then that the church received a letter from our friend and mentor Paul. He wrote from his prison cell to encourage and strengthen us in our times of trial.

Paul told us to 'dig deep'. "Be strong and hold firm to the truths that you've been given." He informed us we should put on the metaphorical armour of God and stand against the forces of evil that try to drag us under. He explained that our struggles are not really physical battles, but spiritual. "They will try to prise open the crack between God and his people. The gulf bridged by Christ's death on the cross is growing again; you must stand and be ready," Paul said.

"Buckle on a belt, to symbolise truth; tie it around your waist, and with it set in place the chainmail of righteousness. It will help you act with justice at the forefront of your mind. Slip your feet into shoes that become for you the gospel of peace, to guide your thoughts and words towards peaceful outcomes. Take up the shield of faith that will extinguish the flaming arrows that may be sent in your direction. Put on the helmet of salvation that will protect you and all those who stand with you from all that comes against you when you dare to bear Christ's name. Carry the sword of the Spirit, which is the word of God. It should be used to show love and hope, not judgement and condemnation."

Having reminded us how foolish it would be to go into battle unarmed, Paul then commanded us to listen to our Captain's orders.

"Pray earnestly, my friends, for armour is important but prayer is imperative. Through it, Christ Jesus is speaking to his father on our behalf. He knows our needs. He hears our requests and he reaches out to those for whom we plead. The battle in the spiritual realms has already begun; let us be prepared to stand up and counted for Christ when the time comes."

Pause for Thought

- How do you feel about the concept of a spiritual battle taking place?
- How do you understand the teaching about putting on the armour of God?
- Have there been people in your life who have pointed you towards Jesus?

Action

Think about each piece of the armour of God and what it symbolises. Picture holding it in your hands, then put the piece of armour on, symbolising that you choose to receive that armour from God. Remember during the day what you are wearing and see if it makes a difference to the way you interact with those around you.

Prayer

God of all,
    help me to treat people with love and compassion.
Help me to use your word for truth, justice and hope
    and not for judgement and condemnation.
Help me to do as Paul did and offer hope to all I meet.
As I pray, hear my prayers for those in need and for myself
    as I seek to serve you better each day.
Amen.

EPIPHANY

Never Too Young

Bible Reading

Paul, an apostle of Christ Jesus by the will of God, for the sake of the promise of life that is in Christ Jesus,
To Timothy, my beloved child:
Grace, mercy, and peace from God the Father and Christ Jesus our Lord. I am grateful to God – whom I worship with a clear conscience, as my ancestors did – when I remember you constantly in my prayers night and day. Recalling your tears, I long to see you so that I may be filled with joy. I am reminded of your sincere faith, a faith that lived first in your grandmother Lois and your mother Eunice and now, I am sure, lives in you. For this reason I remind you to rekindle the gift of God that is within you through the laying on of my hands; for God did not give us a spirit of cowardice, but rather a spirit of power and of love and of self-discipline.

2 Timothy 1:1-7

If you have time, it is well worth reading both of Paul's letters to Timothy.

The Voice of Timothy

What do you do when you are told continually that you are too young to serve your God? You sit and wait it out, that's what. You wait until God breaks the deadlock and sends his messenger with your call-up papers. Then people must listen.

My name is Timothy, and my upbringing was interesting. My father was a Greek, and my mother and grandmother were Jewish believers.

They had chosen to follow the ways and the teachings of Jesus Christ, and from birth they encouraged me to do the same.

I was an enthusiastic child, full of energy and ready to share my faith in Jesus with anyone who would listen. I was told about the journeys of Paul all over the known world. How exciting they sounded – travelling by boat to faraway places, preaching the good news of freedom through Christ! I was young though, and time after time I was told to keep quiet and just to listen to those older than me.

Then one day the word on the street was that Paul himself was coming to town. I was overjoyed. I could not contain my emotions; I felt fit to burst! So, I attended the meeting and sat right at the front.

There Paul noticed my eagerness to serve and dedication to prayer, and it wasn't long before I was on a ship with him bound for Macedonia. Young as I was, I would soon become a leader in the new and growing church.

Paul, my spiritual father, moved on and I led the church as best as I could. Not long after, word came that he had been arrested and thrown into prison, in chains for his faith. Then sometime later, the letters began to arrive – letters of encouragement for me and for God's people; words that warned against false teachings and those who would try to infiltrate God's church. Paul inspired us to keep the faith and fight on.

He also set out instructions for worship and how to structure the fledgling church. He told us how to deal with conflict and taught us about forgiveness and moving on. Each letter was addressed to me, "a true son in the faith" to use Paul's words.

Ultimately, we were saddened to hear of Paul's untimely death. But I battled on, clinging to the knowledge that I had been called and set apart for God – to serve him and to share his truth of forgiveness and hope with all people.

Now I myself sit in chains, awaiting certain death. My enthusiasm for the gospel is as strong as it was in the days of my youth though. After all, you are never too young, or too old, to serve God.

Pause for Thought

- Have you ever been told that you cannot do something because of age, colour, gender or any other reason? What do you think God would say about that to you?

- Have there been times in your life when you have been as enthusiastic for Christ as Timothy was? Are you enthusiastic today?
- Timothy was prepared to follow Jesus anywhere, even to prison and death. How far would you be willing to follow Jesus? What is the cost of following him in your life today?

Action

Imagine that Paul is writing you an email of encouragement. What might he say to you?

Prayer

God of Paul and Timothy,
help me to recognise that you can call and use each one of us.
Wherever I find myself,
make me aware that you can use me in your service.
Cause me to be willing to follow you wherever you lead,
and to put my trust solely in you.
Amen.

Also from the Publisher

The Shepherd Spy

Angie McEvansoneya

ISBN 978-1-78815-677-6

The Shepherd Spy is a collection of 12 nativity plays, for children of all ages and for groups of all sizes.

Each play represents a different slant on the Christmas story, with the author's licence as to some of the surrounding details. We look at the nativity through different eyes – those of mice, a young spy of Herod's, the national news channel, the stars and others. Every play has been tried and tested and can be performed in a small church building with a small stage and no curtains or spotlights.

Most children today only have a very limited knowledge of what Christmas is really about. By actually taking part in a nativity play, the story can become a central part of the children's memories of Christmas.

Available from all good bookshops and from the publisher:

www.onwardsandupwards.org/the-shepherd-spy